Learning
FOR
KEEPS

SUSTAINABLE FORESTRY INITIATIVE

Certified Fiber Sourcing

www.sfiprogram.org

RHODA **KOENIG**

Learning FOR KEEPS

TEACHING *the* STRATEGIES ESSENTIAL *for* CREATING INDEPENDENT LEARNERS

ASCD | Alexandria, Virginia

1703 N. Beauregard St. • Alexandria, VA 22311-1714 USA
Phone: 800-933-2723 or 703-578-9600 • Fax: 703-575-5400
Website: www.ascd.org • E-mail: member@ascd.org
Author guidelines: www.ascd.org/write

Gene R. Carter, *Executive Director;* Judy Zimny, *Chief Program Development Officer;* Nancy Modrak, *Publisher;* Scott Willis, *Director, Book Acquisitions & Development;* Julie Houtz, *Director, Book Editing & Production;* Leah Lakins, *Editor;* Sima Nasr, *Senior Graphic Designer;* Mike Kalyan, *Production Manager;* Circle Graphics, *Typesetter;* Sarah Plumb, *Production Specialist*

All web links in this book are correct as of the publication date below but may.have become inactive or otherwise modified since that time. If you notice a deactivated or changed link, please e-mail books@ascd.org with the words "Link Update" in the subject line. In your message, please specify the web link, the book title, and the page number on which the link appears.

PAPERBACK ISBN: 978-1-4166-1085-4   ASCD product # 111003 n11/10
Also available as an e-book (see Books in Print for the ISBNs).

Quantity discounts for the paperback edition only: 10–49 copies, 10%; 50+ copies, 15%; for 1,000 or more copies, call 800-933-2723, ext. 5634, or 703-575-5634. For desk copies: member@ascd.org.

Library of Congress Cataloging-in-Publication Data

Koenig, Rhoda, 1942–
    Learning for keeps : teaching the strategies essential for creating independent learners / Rhoda Koenig.
       p. cm.
    Includes bibliographical references and index.
    ISBN 978-1-4166-1085-4 (pbk. : alk. paper)
 1. Effective teaching. 2. Language arts. 3. Reading. 4. Cognitive learning. I. Title.
    LB1025.3.K65 2010
    371.39—dc22
                                                                      2010029133

20 19 18 17 16 15 14 13 12 11 10   1 2 3 4 5 6 7 8 9 10 11 12

DEDICATION

For Carol Pufahl
You taught us with such grace.

Learning
FOR
KEEPS

ABOUT THE AUTHOR

Rhoda Koenig's career in education encompasses being a classroom teacher, an elementary literacy specialist, a staff developer, and a teacher of reading and writing processes in a workshop approach at the graduate level. *Learning for Keeps* combines her broad teaching experience, her commitment to teaching students to be self-regulated learners, and her expertise and training as a teacher educator.

FOREWORD

As teachers striving to meet the challenges of the 21st century student, we recognize the need for good GPS systems in our classrooms. In *Learning for Keeps,* author Rhoda Koenig provides a "cognitive" GPS system. In this book, teachers are challenged to think about how they want to lead their students and help them build the literacy and problem-solving skills that are important both in school and in life. In addition to these skills, Rhoda also emphasizes the need for students to develop the attitudes, dispositions, and habits of mind that will help them develop into lifelong learners.

As with any good navigation system, there are twists and turns along the way. But Rhoda provides such accurately scripted and well-described lesson plans, tips, and advice, you feel as if you are in the classroom with the teachers learning what they are doing. What is unique about *Learning for Keeps* is the access you get to Rhoda's metacognitive processing. She reveals her choices, why she made them, and, upon reflection, how she might consider making different choices. This book provides an excellent model for reflective practice and will serve teachers who have been in practice for many years as well as those who are just entering the profession.

Although we frequently hear the rhetoric "all kids can learn," we rarely get a book that so explicitly provides a road map for how to make that happen. *Learning for Keeps* takes us through powerful examples and lessons that model for teachers how they can help students navigate the turbulent waters of becoming independent readers, writers, and problem solvers. Although Rhoda focuses largely on literacy, the practicality of her methods and strategies are applicable to any subject area. Her book is designed as a model for what she professes—explicit discussions about what you want the learner to know, models and examples that clearly define what you are teaching, applications that demonstrate the work at hand, and finally, encouragement to try the strategies in the classroom.

As I read *Learning for Keeps,* I thought about the dozens of students and teachers who will benefit from receiving a final copy of this book. This is one of those books where I found myself regularly nodding my head in agreement. It also brought to the forefront noted researchers and practices that are a vital part of my work.

A book that focuses on cognitive development could be foreboding. You might fear that this will be another work that keeps the brain in the laboratory rather than in the realities of the classroom. Fear not—*Learning for Keeps* is so real that it can easily serve as a field guide!

Bena Kallick

PREFACE

Apparently the case for teaching cognitive, procedural knowledge must be made convincingly and pragmatically. Owing to an explosion of scientific, cognitive, and educational research, we have known about the efficacy of strategy instruction for decades, yet it is the delivery of information and the preparation for assessments that still garner most of the time in today's classrooms.

The explanation is not hard to find. Teaching the learner how to learn as well as what is to be learned takes time. We are constantly battling time constraints in our classrooms. High-stakes testing preparation has become a non-negotiable priority in most schools. In addition, the elementary school day is fragmented and frazzling. Pull-out programs leave teachers with precious few blocks of time in which their whole class is intact and available for a shared experience, the introduction of new topics, and the structuring or planning of activities. In most secondary schools, classes are circumscribed by class periods, and there is no continuity from one instructional block to another. The pressure to beat the bell and cover curriculum trumps lateral learning.

Even if those time constraints and test pressures were miraculously lifted, the preparation and training required for rethinking and shifting from content-driven to learner-driven teaching have not sufficiently pervaded the syllabi of our colleges and universities. Instead, we rely largely on the workshop, in-service model for staff development. Playing catch-up, however, has yielded only sketchy progress at best.

So what is a teacher to do when faced with the decision to either cover material and move on or cover less material in order to engage learners in lessons and dialogue that inform their thinking, enhance their problem-solving ability, and strengthen their key literacy behaviors? Conversely, how does a teacher opt for a practice test booklet once he has seen his students mentoring each other on how to organize their personal narratives?

It occurred to me that some really bright folks in Silicon Valley could help us answer these questions. Listen to Eric Schmidt, CEO of Google; Jeff Bezos, founder and CEO of Amazon; Steve Jobs, cofounder of Apple Computers; Marissa Mayer, Google's Vice President for Search Products and User Experience; and Reid Hoffman, innovator and creator of LinkedIn.com. These individuals and many others are shaping the future of the world, keeping the United States competitive in the global economy, and continually searching for ways to create technology that will enhance our lives. They work and think *process*. Ask them how an innovation comes to life, and you don't hear anything about studying for tests or memorizing information.

The engineers at Google are given 20 percent of their normal work week not to work. It is in that space that they just *think about ideas* they find interesting. Those interesting ideas find their way back to the conference table for further *exploration* and *discussion*. A group of engineers then works up a *strategic analysis* and *draw up maps* that are used to build a prototype. *A team is put together* to guide the prototype into production. Then each part of the new technology is *evaluated*, tried, and evaluated again. Once *feedback is gathered*, marketing *strategies are planned*.

Listen to the language embedded in their exuberance as they describe their work. They are asking questions, searching for ideas, gathering facts, making comparisons, defining missions, building teams, building a knowledge domain, and creating a culture of empowerment to make decisions. That is the work of the 21st century. The unavoidable truth is, those processes are the lifeblood of any innovative, viable organization or discipline today.

Our commitment to creating an environment for teaching the processes of learning and problem solving is timely and critical. It is my hope that this book will help you visualize how to make such an environment a reality in your work.

ACKNOWLEDGMENTS

I didn't really choose to become a teacher. That is why I always considered myself blessed that the career path I wandered onto when I was in the second grade, and in the habit of playing teacher with my little blackboard and chalk after school, led to work I truly loved and felt passionate about. It was a career, after all, that was somewhat preordained for a girl growing up in the 1950s if she was not going to become a nurse or a secretary.

I, however, have been doubly blessed because the work I care deeply about took place and flowered in a collaborative community with esteemed colleagues and valued friends. It is to that outstanding group of bright, dedicated professionals that I am deeply grateful. Sandra Glickman, Elaine Hoffspiegel, Harriet Harris, and Joan Vanecek shared in the vision of empowering students to be self-regulated learners and brought their skills to the mission of making that goal a reality in their schools.

My long-time colleagues at Vanderbilt School were nothing short of extraordinary. Marge Ricci, Peggy Cunningham, and Carol Korobow were a constant source of friendship, joyfulness, daily dialogue, and problem-solving support. They envisioned *my* writing of this book long before I did. I will forever be indebted to Marge for her generosity of spirit when I was the new kid on the block. It was watching and listening to her do her magic with remedial reading students that I first understood the difference between teaching the learner and not just the learning.

To Bena Kallick, the lighter of the flame, and Esther Fusco, mentor and cheerleader, I owe my vision and my belief in what is possible in our schools. They inspired me at many a turn during my long career. A special thank you to three dear friends: MaryTherese Croarkin for reading my early draft with an editor's eyes and giving me the feedback and guidance I needed to correct course and move forward; Carol Pufahl for her exquisite teaching gifts, the insight she brought to the reading of my proposal, and her enthusiastic offer to create a study group; and Eileen Sharaga, my childhood friend, for being there and knowing me.

ASCD publications and conferences have made an immeasurable contribution to my professional development. I am grateful that I was able to place my book in ASCD's hands. I am indebted to editors Carolyn Pool and Julie Houtz for their wisdom and kindness.

I give special thanks to my loving family whose presence in my life makes me strive to find the best in myself. To my children Susan, Robert, and Anessa, thank you for the light in your eyes when I talk about this book and other things that turn me on. To Hailey, Jillian, Rebecca, and William for the bubbles you make in my soul. To Howard, my number one cheerleader and constant techie support, I am grateful.

INTRODUCTION

Just about the best thing that could happen to a teacher who has been teaching for many years is to get a good whack on the side of the head. And that is what happened to me one day in 1986 when I attended a one-day conference at my school district's Teachers' Center. Bena Kallick, a nationally recognized educator, writer, and consultant, was the individual who delivered the aforementioned whack. She was talking about teaching critical and creative thinking. She gave us a brief history of the work that had been going on in the field of cognitive psychology since the early 1970s. She explained how the advent of magnetic imaging devices had opened a window into which researchers could see how the brain responds to different cognitive stimuli. As a result, theories based on observable data were becoming available, theories that could be used to inform our teaching.

That greater understanding of the dynamics of learning and information processing contributed to the reconceptualization of human intelligence. The accepted view that intelligence is something measured by IQ tests—measurements acquired from a performance on a given day, at a given time, on a given set of tasks—was no longer compatible with the growing field of research and study. The work of Robert J. Sternberg (1985) and others maintained that IQ tests are very narrow prisms through which to view intelligence. A more functional and relevant way to conceptualize intelligence, they proposed, is to focus on what one does when one does not know. They recognized that the marks of true intelligence are being able to solve problems; pose cogent questions that lead to exploration and discovery; make good judgments in the light of evidence and information; see connections and apply new learning. In short, intelligence is mental self-management.

I was dismayed to realize I had never questioned the notion that a number derived from a test can assign an individual to a category of high, average, or low intelligence with the indelibility of a laundry marker. But that was not the only profound idea I encountered at the presentation.

I was introduced to the landmark work of Reuven Feuerstein (1980), an Israeli psychologist who demonstrated and documented that human intelligence is modifiable. Although the notion that our IQs are largely predetermined and fixed by the time we reach school age was deeply ingrained in our minds and our classrooms, Feuerstein had shown the contrary. Working with children who had been severely deprived and traumatized during the Holocaust as well as individuals who were designated as retarded, he showed that use of the instructional strategies he had developed could significantly improve his students' intelligence.

I knew, as a teacher of reading and writing, that I could modify my students' behaviors in those areas by mediating their interaction with text. Using a great deal of structure, appropriate pacing, varied questioning techniques, demonstrations, and positive feedback, I was able to help my students become more accurate, thoughtful, and responsive readers and more focused, organized, elaborative, and proficient writers. This new knowledge pushed back the edges of my concept of what I could accomplish with my students. I had more to learn about modifying cognitive behaviors, and I had a lot to learn about teaching my students how to exercise the mental self-management of the behaviors that are essential for a high level of competence and self-direction. That was the whack on the side of the head.

To learn more about teaching for thinking, I dove into the ASCD publication entitled *Developing Minds* (1985) edited by Arthur L. Costa (and now in its third edition, 2001). The theories and paradigms that I read in that anthology and the readings they led to germinated the practices in this book. For me, the most significant influences were Annemarie Sullivan Palincsar and Ann Brown's and Barry Beyer's models for direct instruction; Arthur L. Costa's models for intelligent behaviors (later renamed Habits of Mind), techniques for teaching thinking, and information processing; Robert Sternberg's theory of intelligence; Arthur Whimbey's writings on precise processing and higher-order thinking; David Perkins's work on teaching for understanding and teaching for transfer; Reuven Feuerstein's cognitive modifiability; Esther Fusco's cognitive matching; Lev Vygotsky's social cognition; Robert J. Marzano's paradigm for dimensions of thinking and his explanation of executive control; and Leslie Hart's linking of brain research and learning.

Those teachers challenged me to rethink my objectives and revise my methods in conjunction with the ideas that I used and valued: Frank Smith's conceptualization of reading as a psycholinguistic process; Ken and Yetta Goodman's clarifying distinction between reading errors and miscues; Lucy Calkins's writing workshops, minilessons, and conferencing behaviors; Dale Johnson and P. David Pearson's presentation of semantic mapping for teaching vocabulary concepts; Regie Routman's substantive extended reading activities; Marie Clay's language for observing young learners; Constance Weaver's constructivist approach to teaching grammar; Ellin Oliver Keene and Susan Zimmermann's comprehensive and nuanced reading strategy units; Roger Johnson and David Johnson's structures for cooperative learning; and Brian Cambourne's whole learning.

The teaching techniques described in this book evolved over 14 years while I was working with my primary and intermediate students in our reading room. They were examined and articulated while collaborating with my colleagues in their classrooms. They were extended to in-service workshops for districtwide use with a gifted group of colleagues and adapted for a wider audience while working with my graduate students, who provided further feedback and affirmation. Regardless of the venue, that journey invariably confirmed that turning students on to the power of their own intellect and demystifying complex processes so students could know what to do when they don't know, translates into confidence, competence, and autonomy that generates enough energy in students and teachers to eliminate the need for fossil fuels.

An interesting thing happens between the covers of this book, on the way to designing explicit mediation lessons. After we have clarified the tenets of transactional teaching; articulated the dynamics of changing complex behaviors; learned how to analyze the tasks students need to learn; crafted the scaffolded lessons we will teach; identified and elaborated on the key strategies essential to proficient reading, writing, and problem solving; and reviewed our options for researching our students' understanding and competence, we can step back from our labors and find we are standing in front of a broad canvas.

In the foreground of our picture are the idiosyncratic learner and a teacher thoughtfully, analytically, and empathetically designing instruction grounded in the intention to nurture self-regulated, thoughtful, undaunted learners. However, within the borders of our canvas there is a meshing of forms that brings to mind Picasso's landmark painting *Ma Jolie.* The forms on our canvas are also monochromatic and interconnected. Their common theme and purpose is student empowerment.

We are looking at a classroom in which the teaching of process—how to read, write, and think—is seamlessly combined with the teaching of subject matter. Students are engaged in problem solving and projects that are relevant and appropriate to their needs and interests. Instruction is differentiated according to demonstrated needs and takes place in a flexible environment where students are taught in whole-class, small-group, triad, pair, and individual settings. A sense of community pervades the ongoing reading and writing workshops, in which students read informational and literary texts, write with purpose and passion, conduct research, and delight in resolving their cognitive dissonance with peer and teacher support.

We see a teacher who thrives on reflection and collaboration. She alternates between performer, purveyor of information, model, coach, researcher, facilitator, and evaluator. Her instruction is aligned with current information regarding cognitive development, brain theory, and language acquisition. Her lessons are scaffolded so that she continually and gradually releases responsibility and control to her students. She is mindful of the power of her questions—at times clarifying, at times opening dialogue and extending thought. The feedback she provides her students empowers them by creating opportunities for generating options and making decisions. She knows that in order for teaching to be transformative, it must be explicit: intentional, purposeful, and clearly articulated. In order for that teaching to be useful, must complete the job by facilitating her students' initiation, application, and transfer of learning.

We are observing students who know that taking time is not wasting time. They engage in reflective, metacognitive behaviors throughout the school day. They have a repertoire of cognitive strategies and tools for organizing and processing ideas and information, including graphic organizers, note-taking skills, and journals. They monitor their learning and know how to work cooperatively to answer questions and solve problems. They acquire competence and proficiency while in the process of accomplishing meaningful goals. They engage in self-evaluation and use rubrics that reflect the purposes of their learning. They learn strategies for taking formal tests but understand that intelligence is really measured by what you do when you don't know.

By the end of the book, I have painted a landscape of 21st century classroom instruction. In fact, the last chapter provides an amalgamated snapshot of a day in the life of a class in which explicit transactional mediation of cognitive strategies is embedded in the curriculum. The reader may prefer to visit the long view provided in Chapter 10 first, and then read the other chapters to study details—much as one might prefer to gaze on a painting first from a distance and then step closer to examine the brushstrokes and use of color.

LAYING THE FOUNDATION FOR MEDIATION THAT MAKES A DIFFERENCE

Bringing about transformative changes in our students' cognitive behaviors requires some introspection on our part. We first have to check the efficacy of our core beliefs and teaching practices. This chapter focuses on three orientations to teaching that are essential for the development of substantive improvement in our students' reading, writing, and problem-solving behaviors. Looking beyond the goal of reaching a higher level of literacy, we are about to chart a course for mediation that taps into what is unique about each of our students and brings out their capacity to be self-guided thinkers and problem solvers.

Replacing Transmission Instruction with Transactional Instruction

The professor of my graduate reading course, an aging academic rock star, cast his sweeping gaze over the two dozen young women assembled before him as if he were searching the night sea for floundering vessels. And floundering we were. "Why do you teach reading the way you do?" he had demanded. When the absence of a response was clearly established, he began a systematic inquisition.

Beginning at one tip of the squared configuration of tables, he positioned himself in front of each student, looked her squarely in the eyes, and waited. One by one came the barely audible words "I don't know." Some, myself included, managed to embellish. "I use the basal reader I was given. My principal gave us guidelines to follow for students reading below, on, and above grade level."

That scene and my professor's question (circa 1965) have stayed with me throughout my long career as a teacher, their implications too profound to dismiss. We were practicing teachers who had not taken the responsibility to explore our instructional options and make choices that would be in the best interests of our students. Were we not curious enough, not caring enough, or just ignorant in a domain that demanded our expertise?

I believe another reason explains our disturbing responses that day. Viewing teaching as an act of faithfully following a teacher's edition is a legacy that can be traced to Edward Thorndike, who in the 1920s espoused the theory of behaviorism. He derived his philosophical principles or "laws of learning" from behavioral psychologists and his own laboratory experiments with animals (Goodman, Shannon, Freeman, & Murphy, 1988). Behaviorism held a mechanistic view of teaching and learning that was perfectly suited for the social and economic context in which it arose. It was an assembly line model for an industrial age—piecework done for the explicit purpose of producing predetermined products. America needed schools that would produce a workforce prepared for conformity, speed, and competition.

Thorndike's Laws of Learning

- **Law of Readiness:** Learning is ordered; efficient learning follows one best sequence. This principle resulted in readiness materials and the tight sequencing of reading and writing skills.
- **Law of Exercise:** Practice strengthens the bond between a stimulus and a response. The common use of workbooks and skill sheets resulted.
- **Law of Effect:** Rewards influence the stimulus-response connection. Lower-level discrete skills are taught prior to rewarding the learner with actual reading and writing that reflected those skills.

- **Law of Identical Elements:** The learning of a particular stimulus-response connection should be tested separately and under the same conditions in which it was learned. This principle resulted in testing isolated skills that resemble the practice materials the students had completed.

In the "State of Behaviorism," instruction is provided primarily in a lecture/recitation mode. The teacher is the purveyor of information, and students are recipients who are expected to recall and repeat the information imparted to them. A metaphor for this model is the learner as empty vessel to be filled—John Locke's tabula rasa. Content is king, and the teacher's edition, with its neatly sequenced instruction, is the source. The orderliness of this paradigm is appealing to administrators, teachers, and parents alike. The management and monitoring of "learning" is facilitated by the prepackaged materials. The teacher's edition embodies the publisher's sanctification of the curriculum; instruction can take place in a climate of certitude. Consequently, teachers are tacitly encouraged to park their own observations, judgments, and creativity outside their plan books.

The behavioral or transmission model dominated the pedagogy in U.S. schools for most of the 20th century. The inherent simplicity, convenience, and security afforded by this highly structured approach have, I believe, contributed to the failure of other innovations in education to survive and thrive in American classrooms. The notion that teaching equals learning and learning equals recitation and reproduction became as ingrained in the culture of our schools as popcorn in movie theaters. As a consequence, the focus of instruction was the content of learning, not the learner.

Behaviorism, functioning more as a well-worn hand-me-down than a time-worn cherished heirloom, still has a strong influence on teachers and teaching today. To support our students with the procedures presented in this book, we must recognize which teaching strategies stem from the transmission model. Then we must understand why those practices are not compatible with teaching that is committed to empowering students so they can become self-guided learners and problem solvers who can understand, select, and apply the processes they need for expertise and a high level of literacy in a complex and challenging world.

The Case for Constructivism

Whereas behaviorism is predicated on the notion that sensory information "deposited" in a learner will become a part of that learner's knowledge, constructivism is based on the understanding that the sensory information a learner receives will be sorted, selected, interpreted, altered, matched, connected, used or not used, remembered or forgotten.

We can understand how idiosyncratic the processes of learning and making meaning are, with a level of certainty Jean Piaget could only have dreamed of, owing to the brain imaging technologies that have emerged over the last 40 years. Noninvasive techniques called functional magnetic resonance imaging (fMRI) and positron emission tomography (PET) have been used to construct images of the neuronal activity in the brain related to attention, language processing, and memory (Lowery, 2001; Wolfe, 2001). Neuroscience makes a resounding case for the basic tenets of constructivism.

We now know that the brain, starting with the act of paying attention, attempts to match incoming sensory stimuli with information already stored in circuits or networks of neurons. If there is a match, the information makes sense or has meaning. Therefore, although the brain is always paying attention, a student may not be paying attention to what we think is relevant and important (Wolfe, 2001).

Students' perceptions are influenced by stored information. Two different students can perceive the same information differently. A teacher talking about a shepherd may be understood to be talking about a dog to one child and a person who tends sheep to another child. To a child who has no stored knowledge regarding shepherds, the information would be meaningless.

Memory, too, is a product of a series of choices. Patricia Wolfe (2001), writing in *Brain Matters: Translating Research into Classroom Practice,* explains:

> Most scientists agree that memory is a multifaceted, complex process that involves activating a large number of neural circuits in many areas of the brain. The path to long-term memory is shaped by the learner's unique neuronal map. The part of sensory memory that captures the brain's attention becomes "working memory." Working memory allows us to integrate current perceptual information with stored knowledge, and consciously

      manipulate the information (think about it, talk about it, and rehearse it)
      well enough to ensure its storage and long-term memory. (p. 92)

Wolfe adds, "We now know that memory is not formed at the moment information is acquired; memory is not a simple fixation process. Rather, it is dynamic, with unconscious processes (called consolidation) that continue to strengthen and stabilize the connections over days, weeks, months, and years (Gazzaniga, Ivry, & Mangun, 1998)" (p. 125).

    When teaching with a constructivist orientation (see below), we recognize that learning and understanding is a somewhat chaotic process that the teacher participates in but does not control. The teacher assesses how students think and what they understand and then proceeds to support and guide them with questions, additional information, examples, and feedback. When students experience confusion, when they have difficulty constructing meaning from text, when their writing fails to communicate clearly, when they are unable to solve problems, teachers use their observations to plan and provide mediation.

Principles of Constructivist Learning

- Learning involves not the mastery of isolated facts but the construction of concepts.
- Learning is not ordered or linear, even though the teaching may have been.
- Learning is idiosyncratic because learners must construct concepts for themselves.
- Learning proceeds best when learners find the learning personally meaningful in the here and now and when they know they can experiment and take risks.
- Learning proceeds best when it is relatively "natural," as when people want to learn to do something outside school.
- Learning typically proceeds best for young learners from whole to part. As they mature, some individuals will develop the ability to learn from part to whole, in a more linear and analytical fashion.
- Learning proceeds best when others provide support or scaffolding so the learner can succeed in doing things that he or she would not yet be able to do alone.

• Much learning occurs through the observation and osmosis that are facilitated by demonstrations.

• Learning is also facilitated by direct instruction. However, direct instruction typically has the most permanent effect when provided in the context of the whole activity that the learner is attempting and is most effective when offered within the context of the learner's interest and need. (Weaver, 1996, pp. 153–155)

Transactional Instruction

How do the tenets of constructivism inform our practices? Constructivist principles can be actualized in the classroom by using a transactional approach to instruction. At the core of the transactional instruction paradigm is the understanding that learning, as opposed to replication and imitation, arises from a complex interplay of meaning-making transactions between teacher and students. Characteristics of these transactions are as follows:

• Explicit focus on the processes (strategies) of learning
• Thinking, reading, and writing that engages students in meaningful problem solving
• A high level of student engagement
• Teacher interactions with students that support the construction, as opposed to the transmission, of meaning
• Flexible, multifaceted, and balanced responses to text
• A dynamic approach to learning strategies that gradually releases initiation and control to the learner

In summarizing the practices that characterize transactional comprehension instruction, Pressley and Harris (2006) write:

> Pressley, El-Dinary et al. (1992) coined the term transactional comprehension strategies instruction to emphasize that teachers and students often flexibly interacted as students practiced applying strategies as they read. Students in transactional strategies instruction are encouraged to use the comprehension strategies that seem appropriate to them at any

point during a reading. There is dynamic construction of understanding of a text when small groups of children make predictions together, ask questions of one another during a reading, signal when they are confused, seek help to reduce confusion, and make interpretive and selective summaries through a reading and as a reading concludes. (p. 22)

The research literature of the last two decades has consistently confirmed the efficacy of strategy instruction for improving reading and writing achievement. Many of the conclusions are drawn from comprehensive and broad-ranging studies. The specific teaching strategies advocated in *Learning for Keeps* are supported by the positive outcomes reported in these studies as well.

There is also ample evidence that achievement gains resulting from transactional strategy instruction (TSI) are reflected on standardized tests and other measures. In one study, 80 percent of TSI students demonstrated gains on reading comprehension subtests. Direct or explicit instruction has been found to generally produce better scores on standardized tests of basic skills than do other approaches. Research also shows that the increased teacher/student interaction is correlated with increased student achievement. Appendix A contains brief summaries of the most comprehensive TSI achievement studies.

Transactional instruction is one of the two contrasting teaching modalities used in this model for strategy mediation. A teacher-directed demonstration of a strategy begins instruction; a student-centered transactional approach is used for the practice and application phase of mediation. The teacher's focus is on the learner: what processes the learner is using to make meaning, what the learner understands, and what knowledge and interactions the learner will need to overcome the obstacles being encountered.

When a teacher puts the focus on the learner as opposed to what is being learned, the interaction with the student takes on a different tone, a different time frame, a different line of questioning, and a different set of responses. The students' answers to the questions they were asked are the starting point for instruction instead of the end point. Instruction pursues the student's line of thinking in order to clarify and develop strategies. The distinction between the teacher-student interactions that take place when teaching with a transmission approach and a transactional approach is illustrated with the following scenarios in which the teacher is going over numerical sequence problems that the students worked on independently:

Transmission Model

Teacher: We are going to check your answers to the sequence problems you did. The first problem was 2 7 4 9 6 11 8 13 ___ ___ ___. Who would like to tell us what answer they got?

Student 1: I got 10, 15, and 12.

Teacher: Excellent! How many people got 10, 15, and 12? Who would like to tell us how you got that answer?

Student 2: I followed the pattern of the even numbers first so the next even number was 10, and then I did the odd numbers so the next odd number was 15 and the next even number was 12.

Teacher: Well done! Raise your hand if you got the same answer. Let's go on to the next problem.

Transactional Model

Teacher: We are going to take a look at the sequence problems you did. Let's see what we can learn about solving problems when we have to identify patterns to make predictions. The first problem was 2 7 4 9 6 11 8 13 ___ ___ ___.

Student 1: My answers are 10, 15, and 12.

Teacher: Would you think aloud so we could learn the strategy you used to get your answers?

Student 1: I read all the numbers from left to right. I see they go even, odd, even, and odd all the way through. I see the even numbers are counting by 2s. I want to see if that's true for the odd numbers—7, 9, 11, and 13. It is. Now I can finish the pattern. After 13 comes an even number 2 more than 8. That's 10. After 10 comes an odd number 2 more than 13. That's 15. After 15 comes an even number 2 more than 10. That's 12.

Teacher: So what I heard you say was, first you got the big picture by reading all the numbers. Then you separated the problem into parts—the odd and even numbers. . . . You examined each part. You saw the even numbers increased by 2s. Then you saw the odd numbers increased by 2s. Then you had enough information to fill in the missing numbers. How many of you approached the problem the same way? Was there one strategy that you feel was particularly helpful?

Student 1: I think reading all the numbers first helped me to see the pattern.

Teacher: Gathering all the available information is important for any kind of problem solving. The other strategy you used that is also excellent for problem solving was breaking the problem into smaller parts.

Student 2: I got the same answers as Student 1, but I didn't separate the odd and even numbers. I didn't notice that pattern.

Teacher: You used a different strategy and you got the same answer?

Student 2: Yes. I went from number to number to see how much the difference was between the numbers—if there was a pattern. Going one number at a time, the numbers went up 5 and down 3 so that's how I got 10, 15, and 12.

Teacher: So even though you used a different strategy, you also were careful to use all the available information to find the pattern for your prediction.

Student 3: That sounds much easier than what I did. The first thing I noticed was that every two numbers had a difference of 5. There was 7 minus 2, 9 minus 4, 11 minus 6, 13 minus 8, but then I wasn't sure what would come next, so I looked for another pattern and I saw that there were odd and even numbers, and they were going up by 2s, so then I was able to fill in 10, 15, and 12. I checked and those numbers worked with all the patterns.

Teacher: So by being flexible when the first pattern didn't give you the answers, you didn't quit. You found another way to get the missing information. Then you went back to check if your solution worked with the first pattern you found. That kind of checking is really important to successful work. Is there anyone whose work resulted in a different outcome from the ones we have heard?

Isn't it interesting how there are so many different ways to approach a problem? If there are no more solutions to consider, let's reflect on the strategies we used for predicting. We'll be able to use these strategies when we're reading or solving other problems that require predictions.

The Benefits of the Transaction Approach to Instruction

- Students hear how others think and add new strategies to their repertoires.
- Flexible and divergent thinking is fostered.

- Students are encouraged to reflect on their learning behaviors.
- Students learn to overcome superficial and impulsive habits.
- When discussing process, all answers are valued for the insights they provide to students and teachers. There are no "wrong" answers.
- Because responses are not limited to right or wrong answers, risk taking is encouraged.
- Teachers can map their students' thinking and identify the underlying obstacles to understanding and success.
- Challenged students see what other students do when they don't know an answer. Being "smart" is demystified.
- Long-term procedural knowledge takes place even if the harder to retain declarative (factual) knowledge is forgotten. See Figure 1.1 for a summary of the key features of explicit transactional mediation.

Replacing Implicit Instruction with Explicit Instruction

I can still hear the words replaying in my head. I was enthusiastically telling a respected colleague how I had made teaching cognitive behaviors part of my curriculum. I was no longer just asking my students questions that required them to visualize, generate questions, infer, predict, summarize, and synthesize. I was well past my tentative start at presenting lessons to my remedial reading students that explicitly taught them how to visualize, question, infer, predict, summarize, and synthesize. My elementary grade students were, much to my relief, engaged and enthusiastic about learning strategies. I had my hands full trying to keep my formerly passive students from drowning each other out when they were reading and thinking aloud. Their reading response journals and book discussions reflected their expanded awareness. Instead of thinking on a literal level when reading independently, my students were reading between the lines, stopping to organize ideas, puzzling over unfamiliar words, and making predictions.

During our writing workshops, my students' increased confidence in their command of language was evident in their writing and their conferences. Our

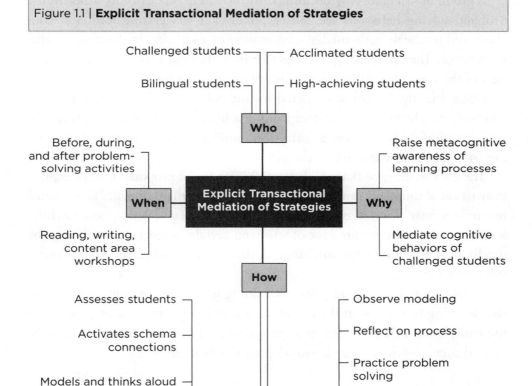

Figure 1.1 | **Explicit Transactional Mediation of Strategies**

explicit explorations of revision strategies had given my students the ability to recognize the need for making changes in their own writing and the ability to work on those changes independently. Some students who had been reluctant to write at all declared they would be writers when they grew up. To my amazement, two of my 6th grade boys abandoned their lunch hour basketball game to come in and work on their personal narratives.

A group of 4th graders wrote and performed a rap on flexibility—one of the problem-solving behaviors we had emphasized. I was getting feedback from classroom teachers; our remedial readers were participating in discussions with confidence. They were using the labels for their thought processes; their awareness of their own thinking was transferring to the classroom.

Consequently, I was not prepared for my colleague's dismissive comment: "Nobody taught me to think, and I did just fine." Was she equating thinking with breathing? Did her words carry the implicit assumption that those who can, do and those who can't, never will?

The early writings of Barry K. Beyer (1985), a major proponent of the explicit instruction of thinking, would have come in handy at the moment. "Educational researchers have pointed out time and time again that learning how to think is not an automatic by-product of studying certain subjects, assimilating the products of someone else's thinking, or simply being asked to think about a subject or topic" (p. 145).

At issue here is the assumption that doing is learning or, put another way, that learning is implicit in the doing. Learning is regarded as a by-product of the completion of a task. This transmission-based belief is often the rationale behind such commonplace classroom activities as these:

- Sustained silent reading
- Comprehension questions after reading
- Workbooks and skills practice
- Test practice booklets
- Weekly writing assignments
- Writing skills exercises
- Grammar and usage practice exercises
- Computation and problem-solving practice

I am espousing a model for explicit transactional mediation that is the antithesis of implicit teaching. As I proceed and explain exactly what those terms mean, you may want to refer back to this list and determine how and why these activities differ from explicit transactional mediation.

At first glance, one would think that the word *explicit* is explicit enough and does not beg explanation; but in fact, there are degrees of explicitness just as there are degrees of strength. To be explicit, the teacher begins by building students' awareness of the strategy. Working with conscious intent, which she shares with her students, the teacher follows these steps:

1. Name the strategy.
2. Explain the importance of the strategy to the students.
3. Relate the new strategy and concept to the students' prior experience.
4. Model the use of the strategy.
5. Verbalize her thought processes.
6. Engage students in reflection.

These teaching behaviors are the cornerstone of explicit strategy instruction and will be discussed in greater depth in Chapter 3. However, following those six steps does not necessarily take our students to the desired destination. These steps to teaching a strategy can be presented in a purely didactic way. Indeed, they can be found in the teachers' editions of many literature anthologies (Rosenshine, 1997). If instruction ends with the teacher-directed strategy lesson, it would most likely not produce the behaviors that are necessary for developing expertise. Excellent readers do not use strategies one at a time, nor do they use them simply when under strong instructional control (Pressley, 2001).

The transactional approach for explicit teaching continues once the strategy is named, introduced, and modeled. The teacher moves on to the problem-solving, interactive phase of mediation in which he coaches his students as they put the strategy to work. When challenges arise while in the process of reading, writing, or problem solving, the teacher engages the students in dialogue in order to clarify and facilitate their use of the strategy being taught in conjunction with other essential strategies (Pressley, 2001; Rosenshine, 1997; Serafini, 2004).

The selection and use of strategies becomes part of the dialogue surrounding the reading, writing, or problem-solving activity. The curriculum takes on a dual agenda of teaching for both process and product. In effect, the teacher invites the strategies to the table and makes them part of the content of learning.

The workshop concept, as first formulated by Lucy Calkins in *The Art of Teaching Writing* (1986) and now a pillar of writing process instruction, is the ideal table setting for explicit transactional mediation. It provides the teacher with opportunities to embed explicit strategy instruction in the minilesson, interact with students in the role of coach and mediator, and place students in groupings that are differentiated on the basis of needs and abilities.

Coaching Strategies at Their Point of Use

Differing from the old paradigm of providing instruction with isolated exercises before and after reading or writing, explicit transactional mediation meets the learner at the point of use. In the way we would help a child learn to ice skate, we would not just give the learner pointers as she is getting ready to step onto the ice and then again when she steps off the ice. To provide the most meaningful and beneficial instruction, we would skate alongside the learner. We would demonstrate, support, coach, give immediate feedback, and let go gradually.

When we function in this capacity, we take on the combined roles of coach and mediator. This behavior is pivotal in elevating students' cognitive functioning. As a mediator we intercede between the learner and the substance of what is to be learned; we are right there between the reader and the reading, the writer and the writing, the problem solver and the problem. As Reuven Feuerstein's (1980) seminal work has shown us, the mediating functions of teaching may make the difference between high and low achievement. As a coach, rather than give advice, hint at answers, or solve problems for our students, we help students analyze their tasks and develop their own problem-solving strategies. Ultimately a coach works to modify another person's capacity to become self-coaching (Costa & Garmston, 2002).

Those of us who followed Calkins's lead in conferencing students' writing learned how to preserve the students' ownership of their writing by asking non-directive questions in a mediative coaching model. Arthur Costa and Robert Garmston's (2002) book *Cognitive Coaching: A Foundation for Renaissance Schools* provides a valuable guide to learning coaching behaviors and informs the coaching responses listed below. These prompts facilitate students' thinking and decision making but do not usurp it:

- Maintaining silence, through wait time and listening
- Acknowledging verbally and nonverbally, empathizing
- Paraphrasing such as summarizing, organizing, and shifting levels
- Clarifying by probing for meanings, specificity, focus, and connections
- Providing data and resources (p. 74)

Here is an example of a mediated coaching interaction with a student who is struggling with the sequence problem shown earlier:

Teacher: So what did you do in order to figure out the pattern and predict the missing numbers?

Student: I couldn't get it.

Teacher: Problems can be challenging. (*Empathizing*) What is the task here? (*Clarifying the focus*)

Student: I have to figure out the next number.

Teacher: Do you have any information that can help you do that? (*Probing for specificity*)

Student: Not really.

Teacher: Have you ever predicted who will win a ball game? Is there information that helps you do that? (*Probing for connections*)

Student: Well, if the team wins games a lot.

Teacher: Oh, so when you make a prediction, you think about what you already know. (*Paraphrasing*)

Student: Oh, I know the numbers that come before the missing numbers.

Teacher: Yes. . . . (*Acknowledging*)

Student: So I'll read these numbers: 2, 7, 4, 9, 6, 11, 8, and 13.

Teacher: So those numbers show you what comes before the missing numbers, and they can help you tell what comes next. (*Connecting*)

Student: They go up and down, higher and lower.

Teacher: Can you be more specific? How much up and how much down? (*Probing for specificity*)

Student: Let's see. From 2 to 7 you add 5. From 7 to 4 you take away 3. From 4 to 9 you add 5. . . . I see a pattern!

Teacher: What are you going to do next? (*Probing for focus*)

Student: I'll use the pattern to fill in the missing numbers.

Teacher: So you figured out how to predict by using the pattern in the information you have. (*Summarizing*)

While we want to be able to mediate the learning of struggling students in response to the needs they demonstrate, we also need to expand our conceptualization of mediation. According to Pressley (2001), "Given the large volume of research on the topic of comprehension instruction in the past quarter century, there has been the potential for a revolution in schools with respect to comprehension instruction. Even so no revolution has occurred. . . . There is a real need for many more school educators to be aware of what they can do to increase students' comprehension" (p. 2). Keene and Zimmerman (1997) searched school districts and universities across the country to see if the proficient reader research was being implemented. They found that the questions and activities used by teachers did little to actually change children's thinking while reading.

Even the students who challenge us to challenge them benefit from explicit instruction. Students who devour books, enjoy tackling problems, and experience academic success can and do eventually hit the proverbial wall. By demonstrating the inner workings of processes that these high-achieving students experience as automatic behaviors, we fortify them with knowledge that they will need when they do not know.

For these reasons, *Learning for Keeps* demonstrates how teachers can provide explicit strategy instruction to all students by embedding the instruction in the curriculum and providing the differentiated support that struggling students require.

Extended Instruction

Explicit transactional mediation is a substantive instructional approach. It is not a temporary repair, specific to the particular task at hand. It is not a prop that enables the student to get the answer being sought, such as pronunciation of an unfamiliar word that has popped up in the middle of a sentence. Such prompts or coaching behaviors are necessary interventions in the minute-to-minute life of a classroom. The explicit mediation we are describing is an articulated, long-term, planned instruction that empowers students to respond to obstacles with confidence and self-direction. (See Chapter 4 for the complete instructional model for transactional explicit mediation and Chapter 5 for sample lessons.)

Learning key reading, writing, and problem-solving behaviors with an explicit transactional approach is analogous to entering into an enduring relationship. There are many layers or stages to work through, and understanding takes time to develop (Beyer, 2001; Pressley, 2001). The first phase of this relationship consists of becoming thoroughly acquainted—learning all there is to know about the new strategy. The learner will need to know what makes it tick, what is unique about it, what can be expected from its use.

In the second phase of the relationship, the focus on the strategy becomes more diffuse and flexible; the focus strategy becomes one of many "friends." The learner spends less time with it but knows when the strategy is the right one to call on; he knows what it can be depended on to do for him. This flexible use of strategies is necessary for expertise (Pressley, 2001). Proficient readers and writers have several processes available to them, and they use them recursively.

In the third phase, the learner starts to take the strategy for granted (but in a good way). The strategy feels natural; it can be used with a level of automaticity— a term Benjamin Bloom (1986) coined to describe the ability to perform a skill unconsciously with speed and accuracy while consciously carrying on other brain functions. The learner knows the strategy will be there and can be initiated when it is needed because it has been internalized. This level of fluency with higher-order comprehension processes occurs over years. Thus, we must conceive of teaching comprehension strategies as a long-term developmental process.

Replacing Inert Knowledge with Dynamic Learning

Practice That Produces Inert Knowledge

I think it is safe to say that the word *practice* has a positive connotation. We have all heard the adage "Practice makes perfect." We know that if you want to get to Carnegie Hall, you have to practice. No matter what you undertake, it is a common belief that the more you do something, the better you will be at doing that thing. Malcolm Gladwell (2008) found, in his insightful exploration of outliers or people whose achievements fall outside normal experience, that doing something 10,000 hours is often the passport to excellence. So it was, in his opinion, for Bill Gates and the Beatles, among others.

Therefore, it is challenging to consider that teachers' confidence, belief, and reliance on practice in the classroom do not always serve our students well. Practice exercises are not an alternative to explicit mediation. The reason for this becomes clear when we draw the distinction between procedural or dynamic knowledge versus declarative or static knowledge. Static knowledge such as facts, concepts, and principles cannot be performed. Rote practice can be appropriate with remembering and retrieving knowledge in these categories. Drilling the multiplication tables, for example, builds memory and makes for quick retrieval and an automatic response.

The term *dynamic* refers to knowledge that is meant to be "executed" by students. Examples of dynamic or procedural knowledge include the following:

- Metacognitive strategies (e.g., planning, monitoring, adjusting, evaluating)
- Cognitive processes and their supporting skills (e.g., predicting, summarizing, inferring, questioning, organizing, elaborating)
- Study skills procedures (e.g., skimming, locating information, note taking)

All of these have a strong performance component. In order for us to use procedural knowledge with automaticity or without conscious thought, practice is essential. However, we witness the breakdown between practice exercises and the actual application of the behaviors. Teachers are often mystified by their students' failure to remember what they practiced regarding spelling, grammar, phonics, punctuation, usage, and comprehension behaviors such as getting the main idea or drawing conclusions. What accounts for that failure?

I would like to stress three explanations. First, practicing dynamic knowledge in decontextualized exercises, such as those found in simulated test booklets and worksheets, does not engage students in the use of mental self-management—the ability to recognize when and how to apply procedural knowledge in a new and authentic context. (More will be said about mental self-management in Chapter 2.) The inadequacy of this kind of practice has been recognized and written about by the most prominent educators of our day. For example, Constance Weaver (1996) explains, "Being able to identify sentence fragments in an exercise written specifically for that purpose does not guarantee that the student knows the critical features of fragments in contrast to grammatically complete sentences, much less that the student can reliably distinguish between the two" (p. 148).

Others observe that when students are provided with information and processes through passive learning and given repeated opportunities to practice, they acquire only superficial, fleeting, and inadequate understanding. The information they are supposed to be learning remains inert. Students are not prepared to monitor their behaviors and adjust their use of skills when they experience difficulty. However, when students are engaged in thinking about and deciding when, where, what, how, and why to apply new learning, their knowledge networks are strengthened and altered. Recognizing when and how to apply knowledge is a crucial catalyst for growth and change (Brown, 2007; Marzano, 2003; Pressley & Hilden, 2006; Rosenshine, 1997; Serafini, 2004).

The second barrier to the effective application of cognitive skills is the students' lack of strategic knowledge. Without a workable plan for executing a skill when it is needed, students are in the position of a person who reads a drivers' manual but does not know how to operate a vehicle. Students need to learn not only what the effective reading, writing, and problem-solving behaviors are but also the strategies or steps that are necessary to put them into action. As Robert Marzano (2003) writes, "Effective practice is not an unthinking execution of a set of steps or rote memorization. Effective practice involves a 'shaping' of the process. This requires a great deal of reasoning about the process and even trial and error to determine process modifications" (p. 116).

A third point to stress is, when students are given practice exercises to learn important skills, they are likely to practice inefficient and nonproductive behaviors and solidify what is not working. Practice will not miraculously transform and elevate. Therefore, although we want students to learn the strategies they need and have repeated and extended opportunities to use the strategies we are teaching them, we want that practice to be preceded by the observation, reflection, and discussion of proficient models of strategic behavior followed by opportunities to thoughtfully select appropriate strategies, as opposed to completing repetitive and predictable exercises.

Working within a transactional paradigm, we first teach the key strategies explicitly. Then we support the decision-making, problem-solving nature of learning. We need to recast teacher-directed lessons so that the emphasis is on the dynamic or strategic aspect of using important skills. The following lesson outlines demonstrate the contrast between these two approaches:

Lesson Objective: Revising Writing to Eliminate Repetitious Language

Inert learning: The teacher makes corrections on students' writing by combining sentences that begin with the same subject, often inserting pronouns, synonyms, and proper nouns.

Dynamic learning:

1. The teacher models ways to avoid repetition, using her own writing. She thinks aloud as she considers options for replacing or eliminating words by using pronouns, synonyms, proper nouns, and sentence combining.

2. Students read their writing aloud to other writers and identify words that have been repeated. Students work in collaboration to select replacement words using the strategies modeled by the teacher. The writer rereads revised work, listening for fluency and clarity.

3. The writer edits subsequent writing for redundant language.

Lesson Objective: Reading with Accuracy

Inert learning: The student reads aloud. The teacher corrects substitutions to be sure the text is read correctly and that the student "learns" unfamiliar or mispronounced words.

Dynamic learning: The student reads aloud. The teacher allows the reader to continue reading after making a semantic or a syntactic error. If the student does not self-correct, the teacher prompts the student by asking, "Did that make sense? Did that sound right?" The teacher can guide the student in the use of fix-up strategies if needed. The reader rereads to maintain meaning before continuing.

Lesson Objective: Understanding Similes

Inert learning:

1. The teacher gives examples of similes.

2. The teacher gives students a practice exercise for matching similes to their meanings.

Dynamic learning:

1. The teacher models how he identifies similes that appear in the text by noting comparisons signified with the words *like* or *as* and noting incongruity (e.g., juxtaposing friends with peas in a pod).

2. The teacher models how he gets the meaning of the simile by using the characteristics of the things being compared and the context of the passage.

3. The students are given text to read that contains similes. They identify and "translate" the similes, working with a partner.

Active Processing and Understanding

Until this point, I have referred to the strategies to provide mediation for as "key" strategies because they are essential to the processes of reading, writing, and problem solving. However, they are also essential to understanding, learning, and memory in a more generic way; being able to employ the full range of cognitive strategies is indispensible to making meaning. Experience has shown me that this is a grossly underappreciated and underutilized concept.

As Bloom's taxonomy illustrates, not all thinking is equal. There are levels of thinking that differ from each other in terms of form and function. Each level must be brought into play in order for new information to be encoded in the learner's brain. Analogically speaking, you could not savor a cake if the ingredients had not first been gathered and then processed by beating or folding or blending before baking. To maximize information processing, we need to identify, clarify, and at times teach thinking behaviors. Arthur Costa and Bena Kallick (2000) clarify the distinction between gathering information (input), making sense out of information (processing), and applying and evaluating actions in novel situations (output).

- **Input** pertains to data-gathering processes, such as counting, describing, matching, naming, selecting, and listing. These behaviors require the least amount of intellectual rigor. The learner is required to make observations at the literal level.

- **Processing** pertains to behaviors that result in making meaning of the information received, such as classifying, explaining, inferring, analyzing, contrasting, comparing, reasoning, summarizing, and synthesizing. This phase is more demanding and requires that the learner actively work with the information. It requires more risk taking.

- **Output** pertains to behaviors that result in the production of knowledge—taking the gathered information, doing something with it, and then creating a new thought or set of thoughts. Examples of these behaviors are evaluating, predicting, speculating, hypothesizing, extrapolating, forecasting, applying, and imagining. This level of thought requires the biggest investment on the part of the learner.

To appreciate why the key strategies discussed here are essential to learning and understanding, it is important to remember that if students do not effectively process information, it will not be consolidated and become part of a learner's working memory. Without this higher-level processing, we succeed at nothing more than adding to our students' "bank" of inert knowledge. As Rosenshine (1997) writes:

> The research on cognitive processing supports the importance of a teacher initiating activities that require students to process and apply new information. Such processing strengthens the knowledge network that the student is developing. Asking students to organize information, summarize information, or compare new material with prior material are all activities that require processing and should help students develop and strengthen their cognitive structures. (p. 2)

As David Perkins (2001) states, "Understanding something is a matter of being able to think and act flexibly with what you know and are coming to know" (p. 446). Understanding, he explains, is not demonstrated by repeating, recalling, or recognizing. Understanding can only be inferred from a performance perspective. Therefore, understanding a topic of study is a matter of being able to perform in a variety of thought-demanding ways with that topic. Depending on the developmental level of the students, they should be engaged in explaining, locating evidence, finding examples, generalizing, applying concepts, analogizing, and representing in a new way. Indeed, the strategies we are preparing to teach are key.

Which Students Benefit from Explicit Mediation?

Learning for Keeps is an outgrowth of my conviction that explicit cognitive strategy mediation is transformational. However, for a more objective story we need to look at the available research.

Reading Strategies Instruction

Research on the efficacy of TSI has been carried out on a wide range of student populations for over two decades. The studies indicate that TSI provides students with an array of strategies, increases their reading comprehension, and helps them develop into independent readers. TSI is a well-validated way to increase comprehension with consistent and striking benefits. The references are available in Appendix A.

- Elementary and secondary students have improved comprehension from TSI.
- Middle and secondary school students that learn to use a repertoire of comprehension strategies increase their comprehension of text.
- High-achieving students have benefited from being taught cognitive strategies.
- Students with learning disabilities learn to mediate their comprehension through intensive, systematic, and explicit instruction in learning strategies.
- Bilingual students improved in decoding and comprehension with TSI.

Writing Strategies Instruction

There is a large body of research in the area of writing strategy instruction. Elementary students with and without learning disabilities were found to improve their knowledge of the writing process and their writing abilities when they received TSI. The following conclusions were drawn from studies of the effects of TSI and writing achievement:

• Students with learning disabilities performed similarly to normally achieving peers.
• Secondary students with learning disabilities increased both the quality and quantity of their writing across three genres.
• Students with learning disabilities, in order to reach a satisfactory level, needed more instruction and more opportunities to write.

Since 1985, the Self-Regulated Strategies Development (SRSD) in writing has been the subject of over 30 studies involving 2nd through 8th grade students in both regular and special education classes. The studies showed

• SRSD resulted in improvements in knowledge of the writing process, monitoring and management of writing, and positive attitude and motivation.
• Improvement was made in writing across a variety of genres, including state writing tests. A majority of students maintained these improvements over time.
• SRSD improves writing of normally achieving students as well as LD students, making it a good fit for the inclusive classrooms.

The Challenges of Transactional Instruction

Although I want to elucidate the benefits of teaching procedural knowledge in a transactional framework, it is equally important to examine the challenges of this approach. If we do not locate and identify those challenges, they could sabotage our intentions just as not charting the shoals of a river could result in running a boat aground. Some of the constraints identified here are subtle and self-imposed; others are products of the pressures we face in today's schools. Experience teaches us that we can surmount the biggest obstacles we face but only via ongoing earnest dialogue, a positive support system, and a good supply of determination.

Teacher Control

The ultimate objective for teaching processes of learning is to empower students so they will be self-guided, confident, autonomous, lifelong learners and achievers. However, in order for our students to gain the control those qualities require, we have to give some of our control away. We have to relinquish the center of the stage and hang out in the periphery while students work cooperatively, teach each other, and make choices that guide their actions.

Some may equate giving students control with losing control. However, the teacher's management and control is omnipresent; it just looks and sounds different. A learning environment that requires the use of flexible groupings, workshops, and peer conferences cannot be productive unless a high degree of structure and clear behavior management guidelines are in place. Modeling, coaching, and assessing are full-time jobs as well. Seeing the earnestness in your students' faces as they engage in seeking answers and hearing the excited buzz of discovery around the room is a great antidote for missing the spotlight.

Conviction

Focusing on cognitive awareness and the explicit instruction of strategies can be an unsettling proposition. Teaching about thinking may seem somewhat ethereal compared to those nice hard facts and sturdy-sounding skills. When it comes to relinquishing the certainty that teaching equals learning, many of us are plagued with doubt. Is it possible that if we don't say it, our students will get it? If we don't grade it, could our students know what they learned and what they still need to learn? Initially it may be hard to believe that raising your students' awareness of their thinking behaviors will translate into their increased confidence and higher achievement on tests. As was cited earlier, the evidence for the gains from explicit transactional instruction is reflected in higher test scores.

A 4th grader named Ruthie helped me, early on, to recognize that cognitive instruction has a quantifiable impact on the learner and the learning. My group of comprehension-challenged readers had listened to me read aloud and think aloud for three consecutive days at the beginning of the school year. By day four they were champing at the bit to contribute what they were thinking as I was reading, so I invited my group of "tween" 4th grade girls to interrupt my reading with their own questions, inferences, and reactions. Within minutes animated conversation was flying faster than messages in an online chat room. When it was time to close our books, Ruthie, wearing the face of someone who had just burst into her own surprise party, exclaimed exuberantly, "I love thinking! It makes me feel so mature!" Ruthie's words and the children's ongoing engagement in their reading were the prelude to an improvement that was reflected in the group's state and standardized assessments.

Paradigm Shift

Making the teaching of process a priority could be thought of as a rescue mission. Learners can become the casualties of content-driven teaching. That realization was brought home to me the day I sat chatting with one of my 4th grade students while we waited for the other children to arrive. I asked Danielle what she had been learning about in the classroom before coming to me. She told me her class is studying the Constitution. "What have you found out so far?" I asked. A look of consternation slid over her face as she searched for an answer. Trying to bring a difficult concept to a concrete level, I asked, "So what do you picture when you guys talk about the Constitution? What does the Constitution look like?" Danielle was stymied. "Did you know the Constitution is a piece of paper?" I asked. "It's a document—a very important piece of paper with writing on it." Danielle's eyes widened as if I had just told her horses can talk.

To resolve the internal struggle between covering material and teaching for the test, on one side, versus thinking aloud, teaching strategies explicitly, and engaging in reflective dialogue, on the other, you could ask yourself the following questions: What percentage of the material that you studied and memorized in the first 12 years of your education were you able to retrieve at the end of that time? How many of the tests that you took during those years could you pass today? Could you have been better served by an education that emphasized processes of learning, concepts, knowledge systems, and defining events while trusting you to acquire specific declarative knowledge in the pursuit of answers to large and important questions? Could the mandated curriculum be presented in a paradigm aligned with genuine understanding and long-term memory?

Change

We all have heard the jokes about change, but the discomfort of changing what we know and are comfortable with is surely no laughing matter. However, if we believe in what the change represents and holds out promise for, we find ourselves more energized than disconcerted.

Making our students' understanding the rudder that steers our instructional decisions is indeed a drastic change from following a course outline. We have to continually research our students' responses and behaviors to make judgments about what our next step will be. Maintaining a weekly plan book becomes an act of clairvoyance. A daily log is more suitable.

When we start out on this path, we may feel like a novice again. We are monitoring our thoughts and words so that we are teaching with our students' understanding and autonomy in mind. We have to build a repertoire of explicit instruction lessons to teach the strategies that are key to our students' success. Collaborating with colleagues and putting a network in place is invaluable. Creating lessons together and sharing the results we get from teaching those lessons makes for a win-win situation for teachers and students. This book is intended to facilitate these transitional tribulations.

Time

Of all the constraints we face when shifting to a dual agenda of teaching process and product, perhaps the most daunting issue is time. When conducting writing workshops with my colleagues in their classrooms, the teachers' reactions to our work with students shared a common narrative: "This is wonderful. The kids are so engaged. I never thought they could select their own topics. The conferencing is really productive. They're actually learning more about punctuation now than ever before because they care about the clarity of their stories. But to tell you the truth, I can't see myself doing this on a regular basis. There just isn't enough time."

Once we make our students' understanding and ownership a priority, the time for process instruction becomes available because activities that do not produce those results no longer clutter the day. Comprehension assessment questions are replaced with students' authentic responses to their reading that reflect their understanding. Rote memorization of state capitals, for example, is replaced with writing and mailing letters to state governors or assembly members to make inquiries or lobby for important causes. Practice exercises in the correct use of quotation marks are replaced with inserting dialogue in personal narratives that are then read aloud or dramatized.

Preparation

The National Reading Panel (National Institute of Child Health and Human Development, 2000) addressed studies relevant to the preparation of teachers in the United States. The study reviewed two major approaches, direct explanation and transactional strategy instruction, and showed the following conclusions:

• Teaching reading comprehension strategies to students at all grade levels is complex.

• Teachers must have substantial knowledge of the strategies themselves, of which strategies are most effective for different students and types of content, and of how best to teach and model strategy use.

• Research on comprehension strategies has evolved dramatically over the last two decades. Investigators initially focused on teaching one strategy at a time; later studies examined the effectiveness of teaching several strategies in combination. However, implementation of this promising approach has been problematic. Teachers must be skillful in their instruction and be able to respond flexibly and opportunistically to students' needs for instructive feedback.

• The direct explanation approach requires teachers to explicitly teach the reasoning and mental processes involved in successful reading comprehension.

• Rather than teach specific strategies, teachers must be able to help students view reading as a problem-solving task.

• Transactional strategy instruction emphasizes the teacher's ability to provide explicit explanations of thinking processes and to facilitate discussions in which students collaborate to form joint interpretations of text and acquire a deeper understanding of the mental and cognitive processes involved in comprehension. (p. 16)

It is to these ends that this book is dedicated.

2

THE DYNAMICS OF CHANGING COMPLEX BEHAVIORS

Lisa

The 5th grade writing workshop is in full swing. A cluster of students are working on their drafts, each in various stages of planning, revising, writing, pencil chewing, and thinking. The teacher is ministering to a case of writer's block. A small group is assembled on the side of the room to share what they have decided are their final drafts. They are following the peer conferencing guidelines that were put in place early in the year.

Mikia, a tall, slender, soft-spoken girl who struggles with expressive language, has just read her piece to the group, and a puzzled pause has brought things to a halt. Lisa, however, is suddenly on her feet and moving to Mikia's side. She is a shy, self-effacing child who is small for her age. Her family has known hard times for most of her years, and her unkempt hair and washed-out clothing reflect that. When she stands next to seated Mikia, their heads are just about level. Lisa leans into Mikia, surveys her writing, and asks, "Did you try mapping? That's what I do to keep my stories from getting mixed up. I'll show you."

Nitsa

The book discussion has ended, and the large group of 4th graders proceeds to read on silently. After several minutes pass, some students begin to make entries in their reading journals, others look back and reread, and some are still reading when Nitsa, a warm, bright-eyed 10-year-old who had been classified as having a language learning disability at the beginning of 3rd grade, pops out of her chair. "So the story goes like this!" she exclaims to no one in particular. Rushing to the whiteboard and grabbing a marker, Nitsa begins to draw the story line. A blue thread emerges on the board tracing the trajectory of the plot, episode by episode, until an iceberg of sorts had been constructed, leaving off at what Nitsa labels the climax of the story.

Noel

Noel, one of the 3rd graders in the group gathered around the conference table, begins to reread his responses to the chapter he just finished reading independently. The page he is examining, in his distinctively personalized journal, is blanketed by a list of sentences composed of crowded, leaning letters.

When he has finished reviewing what he has written that day, he picks up his pencil and begins reading once again. This time, however, he places a letter next to each sentence just outside the thin red margin of his page. "Noel, tell me about those letters you are writing," I say. Noel replies patiently, "Well the P is for prediction, the R is for reaction, the Q is for question, and the I is for inference. That tells what I was thinking. I had lots of questions."

Tennis, Anyone? Learning to Play with the Components of Improvement

Learning for Keeps germinated from the seminal ideas that human intelligence, in all its diversity, is modifiable and all students can grow intelligence. Even if the innovative psychologist and educator Reuven Feuerstein hadn't done his landmark research to which we can point for verification of those theories, teachers demonstrate their belief in the modifiability of behavior every time they enter their classrooms.

When we observe our students' lack of proficiency in some aspect of their reading, writing, and problem-solving behaviors, we have the expectation that we can help our students change and improve that which needs change and improvement. This chapter will examine the dynamics on which behavioral change is based. Relying on our own expertise as mature and proficient learners, we will deconstruct the process of modifying behavior so that we can be effective guides for our students. The sequence of acts that we use to effect change in our behavior will form the basis of our model for explicit transactional mediation.

What Are the Dynamics of Change?

What has experience taught us about the dynamics of change? What are the most useful steps to take when you want to get better at what you do? Whether you want to be better at playing piano or playing tennis, what course of action would you select to maximize your chances for improving one of those complex behaviors? Would you read a manual, schedule more time for practice, or find a coach? The first two ideas pale next to the idea of working with a coach. Why? We must ask ourselves, how can a coach hold out promise for improving our tennis game? What is it a coach does that changes what we do?

• **A coach models.** A coach shows us how a behavior looks or sounds when it is done well so that we can visualize what it is we want to re-create. Visualization is so effective in changing and improving performance, it has been established as a crucial component in training athletes and performers at a professional level. Learning seems to occur by osmosis when we view a pro in action for an extended period of time and then we engage in the same activity.

• **A coach gives feedback.** A coach watches our performance and reflects back to us what we cannot see ourselves. That feedback enables us to become aware of what we are doing well and should continue to do and what we are doing that needs to change.

• **A coach breaks down the process.** A coach views our actions with knowledge and specificity that we as learners do not possess. Coaching clarifies each step or each segment of our actions so that we gain the insight necessary for change and improvement. For example, a tennis coach might show you how far you should bring your arm back before swinging the racket; what position the racket face should be in when it makes contact with the ball; where the racket should be at the end of the swing; where your feet, eyes, and body weight should be at each moment; and what you should do when you have completed your swing. By analyzing the task in this way, a coach raises our awareness to a new level and gives us the clarity necessary for gaining control over the behavior we want to improve. We are no longer just swinging at the ball.

• **A coach guides practice.** A coach gives us ample opportunity to practice. He or she is right there monitoring our actions so that we use the effective strategies we just learned. If we need reminders, if we have questions, if we slip back into our old ways, the coach is still there to support us until our new behaviors become comfortable, natural, and automatic.

These stages of transformative learning can be distilled into five words that represent the dynamics of change:

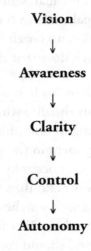

Vision

↓

Awareness

↓

Clarity

↓

Control

↓

Autonomy

By taking the time to focus on a process that needs improvement, providing a model of proficient behavior, and raising awareness of the specific steps required for executing that behavior, we enable students to navigate their use of a challenging strategy. The coach-teacher prepares students for the independent action of a self-guided learner. Metaphorically speaking, such mediation moves the learner from the passenger's seat to the driver's seat. We know from our own experience that as passengers we are much less likely to notice, remember, or care about the route we have taken to get to a destination; we are more likely to need directions the next time we make the same trip. It is not until we take the wheel that we develop the confidence and ability we need to get ourselves to where we want to go.

The Self-Regulated Learner

While the coach is the catalyst for the transformation we are describing, awareness is the change agent. Researchers have found that high-achieving students, at all levels, have one thing in common: they are aware of their own learning. Successful students think about their own thinking (Biemiller & Meichenbaum, 1992; Housand & Reis, 2008).

These individuals know what they know and what they don't know. Flavell (1977) coined the term *metacognition* to label the uniquely human behavior of thinking about our own thinking. When behaving metacognitively, learners develop a plan of action and decide on the strategies that would be appropriate for the task. They monitor their performance by keeping their plan and objectives in mind while they are working. They detect errors and adjust or regulate their actions when the need arises. When they complete the task, they take the time to reflect back and evaluate what they have done. In essence, students who are metacognitive have a permanent, interior coach to pick up where the temporary coach leaves off.

When we listen to these students' self-dialogue, we can differentiate between demonstrations of three different categories of knowledge: declarative, procedural, and conditional.

- **Declarative knowledge:** When students use declarative knowledge, they use factual information to determine what they need to do to complete a task or solve a problem. For example, the student thinks:
  - "I know that a summary is supposed to have mostly main ideas. I have too many details here."
  - "I know I can expect a fairytale to have a happy ending, so I am going to base my prediction on that."

○ "I know this author uses big words, so I'm going to have to take extra time when I read this chapter."

• **Procedural knowledge:** When students use procedural knowledge, they use the information they have about how to perform a task. Here are some examples:

○ "I know that to organize my writing in paragraphs I have to group my details. I better check if I have been doing that."

○ "I know I can probably figure this word out if I blank it out and check for clues in the sentence."

○ "I know how to change *come* to *coming*. You're supposed to drop the *e* when you add *-ing*. I didn't do that."

• **Conditional knowledge:** When students use conditional knowledge they know when to use a strategy and why to use one strategy as opposed to another. For example:

○ "I know I don't usually remember what I read in nonfiction books. I better take notes while I'm reading instead of just reading straight through."

○ "I'm going to map my ideas for my story—that way I can see where to put everything. When I don't do that, I have to go back and rearrange everything."

○ "I just can't keep all these characters straight in my mind. I better make stick-figure notes so I can keep track of who's who."

Although it is evident that metacognitive behaviors are exceedingly valuable to the processes and products of learning, what is not obvious is how teachers can bring about this attribute in all of their students. You may wonder, as I did, whether children are born with a genetic predisposition for thinking about their own thinking in the way they are predisposed to becoming an introvert or an extrovert. The information we have strongly suggests that some people use metacognitive practices without being taught to do so but many do not. Starting around age 5, most children begin to use "inner language." By age 11, some students become capable of abstract or formal thought that requires metacognition, but not all people become formal reasoners, and not all adults actively use metacognition (Costa, 2001a).

Could our instructional practices build on the "inner language" of the young child and foster lifelong metacognitive behaviors? Could our instructional practices inadvertently inhibit or even prevent some students from thinking about their own thinking? The study conducted by Biemiller and Meichenbaum (1992), "The Nature and Nurture of the Self-Directed Learner," clarifies the interplay of factors that have a strong impact on students' use of metacognitive behavior in the classroom.

In a sense, their findings reveal that the rich get richer and the poor get poorer. The students with strong cognitive prerequisites approach tasks with a "surplus mental capacity." This surplus gives them the opportunity to work independently and consolidate their skills, talk to themselves, help others, and verbally review what they know by answering questions. Their less cognitively advanced counterparts find themselves on "overload" when they approach a task. Instead of being self-directed, they go through the motions but are not likely to carry on a dialogue or think about the task.

In addition, teachers and sometimes peers tend to do the defining, planning, and monitoring of activities for the less self-directed students. These children become expert at getting assistance rather than developing their own self-regulatory behaviors. Their learned helplessness, low self-efficacy, and low motivation and engagement have a reciprocal relationship with academic failure (Housand & Reis, 2008). These research findings remind us that the affective components of metacognition and self-direction cannot be divorced from our carefully articulated demonstrations and transactional dialogue.

Growing Metacognition in the Classroom

Teacher Behaviors and Classroom Practices

The explicit mediation procedures in this book provide a model for using metacognitive behavior when teaching strategies explicitly; however, teachers can use several behaviors throughout the day that support and foster the use of metacognitive behaviors as well.

• Teachers have to make room for students to think for themselves. It is challenging to resist the inclination to give instructions for carrying out each step of a task so the end product will be satisfactory. However, when we regard the learner as the end product of our teaching, our emphasis is no longer on preventing "mistakes" in order to "teach" the learning.

• The way we respond to our students' questions and answers can promote metacognitive thinking or shut it down. Affirming answers and giving praise signals students that they have arrived at the desired end point and considering, revising, reflecting, and explaining are no longer necessary. This is fine if you are discussing factual information. However, when your objective is knowledge production, giving a neutral response such as "Oh, I see what you are saying," "Hmm, that's interesting," or "So what you are saying is . . ." keeps thoughts "in play" and encourages the students to consider what their next step should be.

• Questioning students about the process they used to execute a task and solve a problem raises their awareness of the strategies they selected and the behaviors they used to execute them. Paraphrasing, reflecting back, and labeling strategies build awareness.

• Biemiller and Meichenbaum recommend not attempting to achieve equal outcomes for all students all the time so that lower-achieving children are not on "overload" and have the opportunity to extend the dialogue around their work and engage in self-regulatory behaviors.

• Double-entry journals in which students chronicle activities and reflect on the obstacles, questions, and discoveries they encounter foster metacognitive awareness.

Thinking Aloud: The Expressway to Metacognition

Thinking aloud is a transformative teaching practice. Benjamin Bloom's (Bloom & Broder, 1950) intuitive suggestion that two University of Chicago students with some problem-solving difficulties think aloud as they worked demonstrated the effectiveness of this nonteaching practice. Lisa, Nitsa, and Noel, the students described at the start of this chapter, were low-achieving students who were intimidated by every aspect of the reading and writing processes. They learned their reflective behaviors and acquired their confidence as a result of think-aloud practices. Thinking aloud introduced them to the unseen realm of strategies used by proficient readers and writers and motivated them to learn how to execute those strategies themselves.

Since that apocryphal moment at the University of Chicago, *thinking aloud* has become a somewhat ubiquitous term. When we use this practice with the intention to promote metacognition and make the teaching of strategies explicit, some specific guidelines make a difference.

- Thinking aloud should not be a stream of consciousness.
- There should be a clear purpose for the teacher's thinking aloud that is shared with students so they know what they are listening for.
- The think-aloud should be planned or rehearsed.
- When modeling a strategy for students, the teacher should articulate the decision-making aspect of the process.

To focus my students on our curriculum of strategy instruction, I start my workshops each year, regardless of the children's grade level, by introducing or reintroducing all the key strategies experts use. In effect, I invite them to a smorgasbord although I don't put everything on the table at once.

The writing workshop starts out with the class and me working in lock-step. Over several days, I model and think aloud as I go through the processes of selecting a topic, brainstorming or "mind dumping," organizing, drafting, revising, and editing my story. The students apply what they observed to the construction of their own stories. I teach or review the essentials of giving feedback as we go through each step of the writing process. It is the feedback that the students give each other during their writing conferences that reinforces the strategies that have been modeled and taught. This introductory phase of building strategy awareness enables students to see their repertoire of responses expand over time and enables the teacher to make a gross assessment of where instruction is needed.

The reading workshop begins with an overview of proficient reading behaviors. I want students to see that reading is an active, meaning-making process that is not predictable or orderly; the same strategies are used repeatedly and recursively. After each read-aloud/think-aloud, students and I reflect on the strategies that were used and we make a written record of them. After three to five days, the students are invited to interrupt my read-aloud and think-aloud with their reactions to the text. Once the children are actively engaged and reading responsively, they begin reading with a buddy and continue to dialogue about the book. We then transition to independent reading and the use of reading response journals to record thoughts and shape the book discussions that follow. A summary of the sequence of activities suggested for initiating reading strategy instruction is listed below.

Reading Aloud and Thinking Aloud to Initiate Responsive Reading

1. Decide which strategy or strategies you will model in your think-aloud.

2. Select material that is appropriate for modeling the strategy or strategies you want to demonstrate. Strategies could be clustered into ones used before, during, and after reading, writing, or problem solving.

3. Introduce thinking aloud to students. Tell students that people who are successful readers and writers do not work quickly; they work thoughtfully. You want to show them the strategies that help you to read, write, and solve problems by letting them hear what goes on in your head.

4. Tell students you will look down when you are reading (writing) and you will look up when you are thinking aloud.

5. Tell students their job is to listen; when you are finished, you will ask them to tell you what they heard.

6. Prepare students by telling them what part of the reading process they will be observing (e.g., before, during, or after).

7. Record students' retelling of your think-aloud. Prompt students, if necessary, by repeating the things you said. Label the behaviors being modeled.

8. Continue to think aloud for several days, introducing new strategies followed by retelling and labeling.

9. Invite students to respond to the reading using the strategies that have been modeled. Tell them they can interrupt your reading at any time to say what they are thinking as long as they do not interrupt someone else who is speaking.

10. After reading, students retell what strategies they used as they discuss the material. Give students positive feedback on the quality and variety of their thinking. Tell them specifically what you heard.

11. When students demonstrate that they have begun to read actively and use a widening repertoire of strategies, have them continue reading and thinking aloud with a reading buddy.

12. Assess the quality and quantity of students' responses to their reading. When they are actively engaged in their reading, ask them to continue to respond to their reading by recording their thinking in their journals.

13. When discussing responses to literature, continue to label thinking and expand students' field of concern.

Reading Aloud and Thinking Aloud to Introduce Key Reading Strategies

The following is the teacher's script based on the reading of the first nine pages of *Doctor De Soto* by William Steig (1982):

Teacher: I love books by William Steig. He has a great sense of humor but he always has a serious side too. His animal characters act like people. (*Activating prior knowledge*)

• I wonder if that will be true of this book. I would think so. (*Questioning; predicting*)

• Judging from the cover, I would say Dr. De Soto is a dentist and he's a mouse. (*Activating prior knowledge*)

• The way he's standing with one foot crossed in front of the other makes him look very confident. (*Inferring*)

• The picture makes me think of someone who is a know-it-all. (*Activating prior knowledge; text-self schema*)

• I wonder what the excitement or problem of the story will be. I am going to read until I can tell what the story problem is. (*Questioning*)

• Maybe Dr. De Soto will learn a lesson from being a know-it-all. (*Predicting*)

• So I found out after the first three pages that Dr. De Soto fixes the teeth of big animals as well as little ones. When he works on big animals, he uses a ladder or a pulley to get inside their mouths. (*Summarizing*)

- He probably is very confident, or he wouldn't climb inside those big mouths with big teeth. (*Confirming predictions*)
- Oh, I was wrong. He doesn't treat animals that are dangerous to mice. (*Rejecting predictions*)
- I can't believe he and his wife decided to let the fox in. I think he did it because his wife said, "That poor fox," and they probably felt sorry for him. (*Inferring*)
- I'm pretty sure there will be trouble, but we've already seen how clever the De Sotos are. I wonder how they are going to keep the fox from eating them. (*Predicting; judging; questioning*)

I prepared this think-aloud with the explicit intention of raising my students' awareness of before reading strategies that promote interactive and thoughtful reading. The specific thoughts and questions reflect my preview of the book. Although each teacher's think-aloud would be different, they would share the intention of modeling proficient reader behaviors and teach the specific labels for those behaviors. That is the entry level for changing and improving the complex processes of reading, writing, and problem solving.

3

THE INSTRUCTIONAL PLAN
FOR EXPLICIT MEDIATION

The preceding two chapters have stated the case for embedding classroom instruction with explicit transactional mediation. They framed the context needed for this empowering approach to take root and flourish. Here is a summary of the essential components that will be incorporated in the model for instruction presented in this chapter:

- The teacher expects each learner to process information differently.
- Student-teacher interactions build procedural knowledge that the student can apply and transfer beyond a specific activity.
- Strategies are taught explicitly along with the content of the curriculum.
- The teacher provides coaching and mediation during reading, writing, and problem solving.
- Strategy instruction is extended over time to allow students to internalize the strategies being taught.
- Cognitive processing is improved by raising students' awareness of their thinking behaviors with the teacher's use of modeling, thinking aloud, giving feedback, and engaging in problem-solving dialogue.

- Decision making while doing authentic tasks enables students to engage in the mental self-management necessary for acquiring usable, dynamic knowledge.
- Higher-level thinking behaviors are used to foster deep processing of information, long-term learning, and understanding.
- A gradual release of teacher direction and control is used to advance each student from novice to self-directed learner.
- Explicit instruction is provided to all students as an ongoing part of the total curriculum.
- Intervention is provided for low-achieving students by differentiating the time and materials used for their instruction.

The Roots of Explicit Transactional Mediation

Researchers Palincsar and Brown (1984) introduced explicit instruction, the first intervention for teaching students to (1) weave the use of individual strategies together as proficient readers do and (2) articulate the strategies in a self-regulated fashion rather than only on cue from the teacher (Pressley, 2001, p. 5). Palincsar and Brown (1989) defined explicit instruction in this way:

> Virtually all of the instructional research on strategy instruction has certain features in common. These features have been identified with "direct instruction" (Rosenshine, 1979) and include (1) identifying the strategy, (2) explaining why it is being taught, (3) demonstrating its use, (4) guiding students' acquisition and application of the strategy, (5) explaining when the strategy should be useful, and (6) informing students how to evaluate the effectiveness of using the strategy and what to do if the strategy has not been effective. (p. 31)

These six features are embedded in the instructional plan presented in *Learning for Keeps*. Under the guidance of a teacher-coach, those instructional elements create the vision, awareness, clarity, control, and autonomy needed to transform a complex behavior. The relationship between those dynamics for change and the steps for explicit instruction is shown in Figure 3.1.

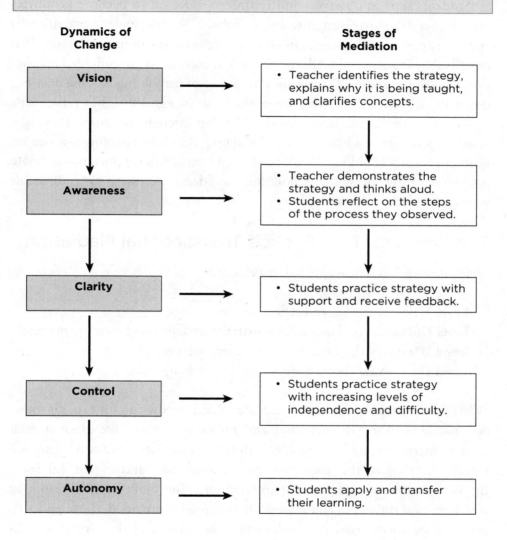

Figure 3.1 | **The Dynamics of Explicit Instruction**

Dynamics of Change

Stages of Mediation

Vision
- Teacher identifies the strategy, explains why it is being taught, and clarifies concepts.

Awareness
- Teacher demonstrates the strategy and thinks aloud.
- Students reflect on the steps of the process they observed.

Clarity
- Students practice strategy with support and receive feedback.

Control
- Students practice strategy with increasing levels of independence and difficulty.

Autonomy
- Students apply and transfer their learning.

Scaffolding: The Gradual Release of Control

Students start as observers and recorders, move on to become neophytes receiving collaborative support, and culminate as independent practitioners applying appropriate strategies in all areas of the curriculum. This model, first described by Pearson and Gallagher (1983), is also known as scaffolded instruction. As Rosenshine (1997) tells us, the essence of scaffolding is "One does not direct the learner, as one does when teaching an algorithm, but rather, one *supports* or scaffolds the learner as they develop internal structures. Providing concrete prompts, modeling their use, thinking aloud, and guiding practice are all examples of scaffolding" (p. 2). Scaffolded instruction supports our ultimate goal of fostering the self-direction and confidence necessary for individuals who can problem solve and create.

The Four Levels of Explicit Transactional Mediation

There are four levels of scaffolded instruction:

Level I: Focus, model, and reflect on the strategy.
Level II: Practice problem solving with the strategy using concrete materials.
Level III: Apply the strategy to a problem-solving task.
Level IV: Transfer the strategy to problem-solving tasks.

What follows is an orientation to the scaffolded instruction for explicit transactional mediation. The activities and interactions that take place at each level of instruction are described, explained, and clarified. (See also Figure 3.2 for an overview of this four-part instructional plan and Figure 3.3 for a detailed outline of each level of instruction.) The brain-based research in which each of the lesson components is anchored is provided in Appendix B, and you are encouraged to supplement your reading of this overview with the information provided there. You will see how these teaching practices capitalize on how the brain works to pay attention, make meaning, process information, learn behaviors, and store and retrieve information in long-term memory.

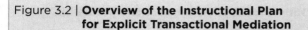

Figure 3.2 | **Overview of the Instructional Plan for Explicit Transactional Mediation**

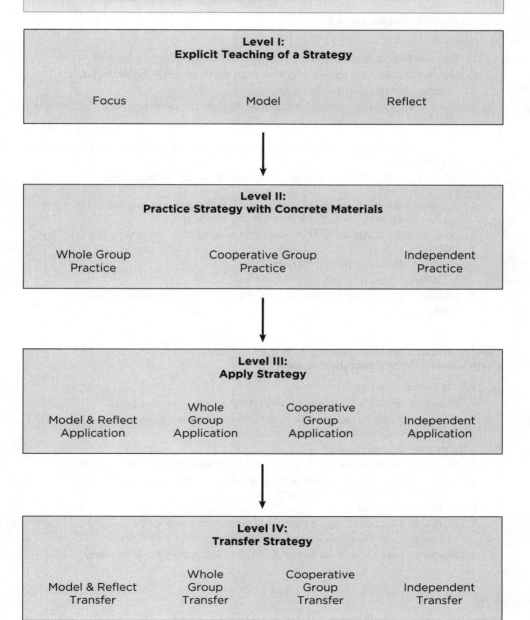

| Figure 3.3 | **The Instructional Outline for Explicit Transactional Mediation** |

Level I: Explicit Teaching of a Strategy

A. Focus
   1. Teacher tells students which strategy they are going to be taught.
   2. Teacher explains or shows why the strategy is important and useful.
   3. Teacher clarifies central concepts.
   4. Teacher makes the connection between students' prior knowledge and the strategy.
B. Model
   1. Teacher uses visual aids or manipulative materials to demonstrate how to use the strategy.
   2. Teacher models think aloud, articulating the steps in the process.
C. Share and Reflect
   1. Teacher asks students to retell the steps of the process they observed and make a written record of the steps in the strategy.
   2. Teacher asks students to think-pair-share-write the answers to these questions:
      a. What strategy are you learning?
      b. Why are you learning it?
   3. Students share their responses with the class and receive feedback from peers and teacher.

**Level II: Practice Problem Solving with the Strategy
Using Visual Aids or Concrete Materials**

A. Whole Group Practice
   1. Students practice the strategy with peer and teacher support.
   2. Students share questions and reactions and receive feedback.
   3. Students reflect on their learning.
B. Cooperative Group Practice
   1. Students practice the strategy in a small group with teacher coaching.
   2. Groups share the outcomes of their work with the whole class, receive feedback, and reflect on the process.
C. Independent Practice
   1. Students practice using the target strategy independently.
   2. Students journal and share responses with teacher and class.
   3. Students take time to reflect and evaluate what they have learned.

Figure 3.3 | (Continued)

Level III: Apply Strategy to a Problem-Solving Task

A. Model and Reflect Application
    1. Teacher models the application of the strategy to a reading, writing, or problem-solving task.
    2. Students retell what they observed.
    3. Students reflect on the process and share their responses.
B. Whole Group Application
    1. Students work with teacher support in applying the strategy to content material.
    2. Students reflect and share responses and questions.
C. Cooperative Group Application
    1. Students apply the strategy to content material with teacher coaching.
    2. Groups share the outcome of their work with the whole class, receive feedback, and reflect on the process.
D. Independent Application
    1. Students apply the strategy working without peer or teacher coaching.
    2. Students share the outcome of their work with the whole class, receive feedback, and reflect on the process they used.

Level IV: Transfer Strategy to Problem-Solving Tasks

A. Model and Reflect Transfer
    1. Teacher models the application of the focus strategy in different contexts across the curriculum and in different problem-solving situations.
    2. Students retell what they observed.
    3. Students think-pair-share-write their answers to these questions:
        a. What did you learn?
        b. Why are you learning it?
B. Whole Group Transfer
    1. Teacher prompts students to engage in the selection of task-appropriate strategies while working in subjects across the curriculum and in nonacademic problem-solving situations.
    2. Students journal, reflect, and share their processes to maintain a metacognitive dialogue and learn from each other.
C. Cooperative Group Transfer
    1. Students select appropriate strategies to complete tasks across the curriculum while working cooperatively.
    2. Students share their processes and products with the whole group, receive feedback, and reflect on the outcome of their efforts.

> ## Figure 3.3 | **(Continued)**
>
> D. Independent Transfer
>   1. Students regulate, monitor, and evaluate their reading, writing, and problem solving by selecting task-appropriate strategies when working in content areas and when problem solving.
>   2. Students maintain process journals, construct rubrics, and receive peer and teacher feedback to evaluate and revise works in progress.

Level I: Focus, Model, and Reflect

Mediation of a key strategy begins behind the scenes with the teacher's preparation for the model lesson and think-aloud (see Chapter 4 on task analysis). The teacher analyzes the strategy to be taught for its component parts. Deconstructing the strategy allows us to do two things: (1) provide students with a clearly articulated sequence of steps that would be lost if we just revealed the products of our thoughts but not our process, and (2) understand the cognitive prerequisites of the strategy that enables us to determine if instruction has to begin at a more fundamental level (e.g., teaching categorization before summarizing).

Level I launches the study of a strategy. It is a three-part teacher-directed lesson that begins by focusing the students on what they are going to learn and why they are learning it. The reason for studying the strategy is explicitly connected to the needs students have demonstrated. The teacher then clarifies the concepts and the terminology by relating them to the students' prior experience (e.g., relating the concept of predicting to forecasting the weather or anticipating the outcome of a soccer game).

In the second part of the lesson, the teacher models how she uses the strategy to solve a problem or figure something out using concrete or pictorial materials. She articulates the steps she is taking and the reasoning behind each decision. Excess verbiage is avoided so that the students can retell what they observed. The strategy being taught is applied to a problem or situation that does not challenge students to understand difficult vocabulary or concepts. Using familiar stories, pictures, or concrete materials allows students to concentrate on the procedural aspects of the lesson.

The effectiveness of using concrete materials for the model lesson cannot be overstated. Not only are the objects attention grabbing, but when they are used to teach a new strategy, they serve as a hook that students can grasp when searching for a strategy to solve a problem. Categorizing assorted blocks, for example, helps students understand the essential concept of organizing ideas before writing. Reshaping a lump of clay clarifies the idea of crafting the design of a story. A pipe cleaner is an effective prop for conveying the concept of flexibility in problem solving. Selecting the missing piece for a jigsaw puzzle demonstrates the use of context clues for inferring word meanings. Hiding an object in a bag and guessing about what is inside fosters an understanding of how prediction heightens interest when reading. Displaying a drawing or a model of a skeleton and comparing it to a story summary can emphasize the avoidance of details in a summary.

My observations of students' engagement when manipulative materials are brought into the left-brain business of concept formation and language comprehension confirmed one of Jean Piaget's teachings (Piaget & Duckworth, 1973) that concept formation is the end product of a series of concrete actions. So when we demonstrate a process such as categorizing and organizing with manipulative materials, we are laying the foundation for the abstract task of categorizing and organizing information and ideas.

A model lesson that introduces a strategy with the use of a visual metaphor (such as the ones listed above), can create a "light bulb" moment for a student. However, in order for students to benefit from metaphors, they must be able to engage in correlational reasoning; they must be able to compare and see the similarity between two disparate entities. From a cognitive development perspective this kind of thinking usually comes in line around the age of 10 or 11. Students who have not entered the stage of formal reasoning will process these comparisons on a literal level and will not make the connections that will enhance their grasp of the concepts and processes being taught.

In the third part of the lesson, students are asked to retell the steps of the strategy. Students and teacher work together to articulate and record the process they observed. When we make a record of our cognitive processes and give them a label, we create a reality for ourselves that we previously did not have. Just think of looking at an animal cell under a microscope in your high school biology class before and after learning to identify the parts of the cell structure or viewing the stars in the night sky before and after learning the configuration of the constellations. The creation of labels is a tool we use to structure our perceptions. New labels foster new perceptions (Costa, 2001b). The last processing activity in the explicit teaching of a strategy provides students with time for metacognitive reflection and journaling so that the learners and the teacher become aware of what they know and what they do not know.

Levels II and III: Practice and Apply

In Levels II and III, students first practice and then apply the strategy with increasing levels of independence. Instruction can be differentiated. Level II begins with the students receiving teacher support to solve problems using content-free materials that are not conceptually or semantically challenging. Then students work, first cooperatively, then independently, using the new strategy to problem solve. The teacher observes and coaches. Reflection and dialogue continues, giving students opportunities to verbalize what they know and what they don't know. Students can create raps, rhythms, or rhymes to reinforce and associate the central features of the strategies they are learning.

Level III begins with the teacher modeling how she applies the strategy to content material. The lessons are embedded in the classroom curriculum. Teacher support is replaced by peer support as students work in small groups, triads, and pairs. Conversations, coaching, and reflection provide opportunities for the teacher to stress the interplay of multiple strategies while reading, writing, and solving problems. The activities that take place center on answering questions of consequence, resolving discrepancies that have been discovered in a text, analyzing information, drawing conclusions, making comparisons, finding solutions, and making decisions. While in the pursuit of answers to these larger questions, students have many opportunities to engage in mental self-management as they must recognize the need to use other strategies they have been taught. For example, students decide how to

- Fix disorganized writing.
- Provide appropriate elaboration.

- Eliminate sentence fragments.
- Improve recall of expository text.
- Get the author's message.
- Locate an answer that was not stated.
- Avoid careless mistakes.
- Find an alternative method of solving a problem.

At the last stage of Level III, students work independently and use their journals to record, reflect, map, and process their problem-solving experiences and difficulties. The journals reflect the degree to which the students have internalized the cognitive behaviors being taught. Blank pages, scant writing, partially accurate statements, well-elaborated thoughts, noted discrepancies, questions, and discoveries inform both the student and the teacher.

Level IV: Transfer

In Level IV, students are taught to transfer and apply their learning to new contexts. The teacher coaches students as they identify the demands of problems that arise in completing academic and nonacademic projects and guides them to select strategies that would be appropriate. Planning events such as an author's tea or a science fair are opportunities to apply strategies for predicting, inferring, being thorough and accurate, organizing, and questioning.

Some readers might wonder, Wouldn't explicit mediation take away from the joy of authentic reading and the creativity of writing? I have found the inverse to be the case for several reasons. The model's lessons engage students of all ability levels. Reading and writing takes place in an energizing environment of problem solving, student ownership, and collaboration. The higher-order thinking required for the substantive exploration of a text or a peer's writing results in students making deep, meaningful, and long-lasting connections. Students who have difficulty reading and writing well are energized by the control they experience when they no longer feel overwhelmed or confused.

Creativity and having a solid foundation of skills and knowledge are not mutually exclusive. Picasso studied classical painting as a beginning artist. Before he turned the art world upside down he did studies of fingers, feet, and faces. He learned techniques for creating perspective, contour, and balance. When we give students the instruction that strengthens their reading, writing, and problem solving performances, we empower them with competence and confidence so that, like Picasso, there is no limit to where they can go.

Deciding How to Pace Explicit Instruction

Pressley (2001) stated, "There is increasing awareness that teaching of comprehension strategies has to be conceived as a long-term developmental process" (p. 7). There is a threshold of experiences over which a student must cross before a new, consciously executed process becomes an automatic response to a problem initiated by the student. That threshold varies from learner to learner.

Pacing is important. Each strategy should be given time to evolve, "ripen," and meld with other strategies over a period of several weeks. Strategy mediation yields cumulative benefits to students when it is part of the life of a classroom. When teaching is explicit, when students' responses are used to inform the progression of the instruction, when practice is ongoing and applied in different contexts, the cognitive behaviors we teach translate into learning that our students walk out the door with.

4

TASK ANALYSIS:
CRAFTING EXPLICIT MEDIATION

Providing explicit mediation requires some detective work. When students habitually experience difficulty reading, writing, or problem solving, it is usually not because one specific behavior eludes them. They are usually overwhelmed because they do not grasp the underpinnings or prerequisites for a complex set of behaviors. For example, we may observe that when David, a 4th grader, tries to summarize what he has read, he retells everything he can remember. We would probably agree that David either does not understand the concept of summarizing or needs to learn a strategy for chunking information. However, to teach him that strategy, he may need to learn one or more supporting skills, such as learning to discriminate between topics and details, understanding and labeling the relationship between topics and details, and inferring an unstated topic from the stated details. Since those supporting skills are contingent on the cognitive prerequisites of being able to classify and categorize information, David may need to learn to recognize and apply those organizing skills.

David's inability to summarize would probably preclude his ability to synthesize information, get the author's message, and organize ideas for improved recall. All of these behaviors rest on applying classification and categorization skills, the same cognitive prerequisites necessary for summarizing. He would have to understand and discriminate between super-ordinate and subordinate ideas. Our model for explicit teaching enables us to focus David's instruction on his specific cognitive and procedural needs.

Through mediation, we can clarify our students' thinking. We can thoughtfully, deliberately, and proactively help developing learners. For those who demonstrate confusion, lack of proficiency, inaccuracy, frustration, avoidance, and affected boredom, we can, in effect, stop the bus so that they can get on. We can identify and isolate each problem that challenges them and shine a bright, illuminating light on those problems.

Why We Start with Task Analysis

To appreciate why task analysis is essential for effective mediation, we have only to put ourselves in the position of the learner in a new and challenging situation. Taking a word-processing course was my Waterloo. It was of no small consequence that I lacked confidence in my ability to tame the computer beast. I was devoid of essential prior knowledge and unable to comprehend a large percentage of computer terminology—a scenario not at all dissimilar to what inexperienced learners may encounter in our classrooms.

Then there was the manner in which I was being taught. Keys were hit, a mouse was clicked, words were spoken, and in the end I was no more able to perform the operations I was trying to learn than before I began. What was wrong with that picture? What did I need from my teacher? What would have served me better? My instructor was modeling the process for me, which was a good thing, but the pace was too fast. I could not differentiate the parts of the new procedure; no sooner had one step been taken than the next one was under way.

No attempt was made to check in with me to see how I was processing the demonstration while it was in progress. It was assumed my brief exposure to the way things were done would suffice. I was not given an opportunity to practice what was taught; the instructor stayed in the driver's seat. When the demonstration was over, I had no more clarity than when it began.

We face a challenge, however, when we set out to model a strategy for our students; that challenge is our own proficiency. Most of the procedures we use when we read, write, and solve problems seem to occur effortlessly. We tend to be much more focused on the outcome of our efforts than we are with the processes we use. As Patricia Wolfe (2001) noted

> The famous cognitive psychologist Jerome Bruner called procedural memory *a memory without record* (Squire & Kandel, 2000). The automatic procedures form a sort of unconscious stimulus-response bond. Once we have a skill or habit at this level, however, it becomes difficult to access it in any way except by performing it. Imagine trying to teach someone to tie a shoe, swing a golf club, or write a word without physically demonstrating it. We no longer know how we accomplish the procedure. Its separate parts or its rules of operation are virtually inaccessible to our consciousness. (Wolfe, p. 114)

In order for us to demonstrate a strategy to our students, which we experience as spontaneous and instinctual, we have to be adept at paying attention as we work; we have to slow down our actions and isolate each step we take. In other words, we have to be able to analyze the task we want to teach.

Slowing Down the Process

When we analyze a task, we take the whole of a strategy and reduce it to its component parts. We rely on our deductive reasoning ability in the same way we do when we plan an event such as a party. We work our way backward from the idea of the party to identifying the steps we need to take in order to make it happen. Thoroughness counts. We would not be satisfied with the outcome if our plans didn't include invitations, food, drinks, extra chairs and tables, plates, napkins, utensils, serving pieces, glasses, music, entertainment, arrangements for out-of-town guests, and so on.

So analyzing a task requires starting at the end point—the goal—and then deconstructing the steps it takes to get there. A suggested process for task analysis follows:

1. Visualize an audience that has no prior knowledge of the task.
2. Work through the task and verbalize everything you are thinking and doing.

3. Make a written record of what you are saying as you are thinking aloud.

4. Use your list of specific responses to extrapolate the steps of the process you use.

It is helpful to have a partner to act as an observer and recorder while you are using the focus strategy and thinking aloud, or record yourself. Your list of steps will become the core of your explicit strategy lesson. For the purposes of this chapter we will limit our focus to the analysis and instruction of just one key strategy—inferring. A full discussion of making inferences and the other key strategies appear in Chapters 6, 7, and 8.

Regardless of the specific nature of the inferential thinking going on in the reader's mind and whether the inference is made spontaneously or whether it is being elicited by a question someone else has asked, the underlying structure of the strategy used to make inferences remains essentially the same.

When I set out to excavate a strategy in preparation for my direct instruction lesson, I am doing the kind of ground work an actor does to prepare for a role or a lawyer does to prepare for a final summation. I want to teach myself everything I need to know about my subject. I want to catch myself thinking—in this case, making inferences. The material I read has to be challenging and engaging for me. Using a book I am reading for the first time allows me to observe myself making inferences authentically.

I selected a passage from Marilynne Robinson's (1980) complex and haunting book *Housekeeping* (p. 145). I chose a paragraph in which a major character, Sylvie, is introduced. I thought that passage would give me the opportunity to make inferences about her character traits. I stayed focused on making inferences about the character although questions, predictions, and judgments were bound to pop into my mind as I read. When I finished reading and thinking aloud, I reviewed my responses and extrapolated generalizations that described the process I used to arrive at the inferences I made about Sylvie.

My Think-Aloud

Let's see what I can find out about who Sylvie is.

Sylvie came into the kitchen behind her, with a quiet that seemed compounded of gentleness and stealth and self-effacement.

The author tells us three of Sylvie's character traits right there. By saying she is gentle, stealthy, and self-effacing, I would infer that she has something to hide or feels that she does. That would be unsettling since we already know she is going to become the guardian to her nieces.

Sylvie was about 35 years old, tall, and narrowly built.

This description helps me visualize her but it doesn't give me any ideas about her character.

She had wavy brown hair fastened behind her ears with pins, and as she stood there, she smoothed the stray hairs back, making herself neat for us.

What do her actions tell me about her? The act of smoothing her hair makes me infer that she wants her sisters and nieces to find her acceptable.

Her hair was wet, her hands were red and withered from the cold, her feet were bare except for loafers.

Most of the description in that sentence doesn't tell me anything about Sylvie's character, but the fact that her feet are bare in the winter is striking. I could infer that she is an unconventional soul and she is indifferent to the cold but I associate bare feet in winter with poverty. I've had students who came to school in winter without socks.

Her raincoat was so shapeless and oversized that she must have found it on a bench.

This information about the coat she is wearing along with what I just read makes me infer Sylvie is either homeless or vagrant because I associate the grossly ill-fitting raincoat with people I've seen living on the street.

Lily and Nona glanced at each other, eyebrows raised.

What would make them raise their brows? From what I read, I would infer that these very conventional ladies are surprised and disapproving of her shabby appearance.

There was a little silence and then Sylvie hesitantly put her icy hand on my head and said, "You're Ruthie. And you're Lucille. Lucille has the lovely red hair."

At first the word *stealth* made me infer Sylvie may be somewhat sneaky or not trustworthy, but the rest of the information makes me think she is stealthy in the way someone who has to live by her wits would be. The way she's dressed along with her tolerance of the cold makes me infer she is accustomed to living outside like a homeless person. The way she greeted Ruthie and Lucille was somewhat tentative, gentle, and kind, but I would infer the girls are being entrusted to a complicated, perhaps wild woman. I'm not sure yet.

Extrapolating the Strategy

To elicit the strategy for constructing an inference, I review my think-aloud and group my remarks according to their shared characteristics. Those shared characteristics or generalizations become the extrapolated statements, which describe the components of the strategy.

Think-aloud:
• "Let's see what I can find out about who Sylvie is."
Extrapolation: I wanted to know something that has not been stated.

Think-alouds:
• "The author tells us three of Sylvie's character traits right there. By saying she is gentle, stealthy, and self-effacing, I would infer that she feels she has something to hide or feels that she does. That would be unsettling since we already know she is going to become the guardian to her nieces."
• "That act of smoothing her hair makes me infer she wants her sisters and nieces to find her acceptable."
Extrapolation: I gathered information that gave me clues for making thoughtful guesses about what I want to know.

Think-alouds:
• "The fact that her feet are bare in the winter is striking. I could infer that she is an unconventional soul and indifferent to the cold, but I associate bare feet in winter with poverty. I have had students who came to school in winter without socks."
• "This information about the coat she is wearing along with what I have read makes me infer Sylvie is either homeless or a vagrant because I associate the grossly ill-fitting raincoat with people I've seen living on the street."
• "From what I have read, I would infer that these very conventional ladies are surprised and disapproving of Sylvie's shabby appearance."

Extrapolation: I used information from my own experience and from prior reading to make some of my thoughtful guesses.

Think-aloud:
• "At first the word *stealth* made me infer Sylvie may be somewhat sneaky or not trustworthy, but the rest of the information makes me think she is stealthy in the way someone who has to live by her wits would be. The way she's dressed along with her tolerance of the cold makes me infer she is accustomed to living outside like a homeless person."

Extrapolation: I looked for connections between all the pieces of information. Then I made a thoughtful guess about what I wanted to know that was supported by all the information I'd gathered. I eliminated guesses that were not supported by all of the information.

Think-aloud:
• "The way she touched and spoke to Lucille and Ruthie was somewhat tentative, gentle, and kind, but I would infer the girls are being entrusted to a complicated, perhaps wild woman. I'm not sure yet."

Extrapolation: My inferences are my own guesses based on information; they identify what is reasonably true.

Summary of the Steps to Model When Teaching How to Make Inferences

1. Make inferences when you want to know something that has not been stated.

2. Gather all the available information that could provide clues for making thoughtful guesses about what you want to know.

3. Use information from your own experience and from prior reading to make some thoughtful guesses.

4. Look for connections between all the pieces of information. Then make a thoughtful guess about what you want to know that is supported by all the information you gathered. Eliminate guesses that are not supported by all the available information.

5. Keep in mind that inferences are guesses based on information; they identify what is reasonably true.

Practice Exercises

1. As you are reading a book for enjoyment or for information you need, monitor yourself for questions that arise in your mind. Select one of those questions—for example, a question that involves character motivation, the author's point of view, visualization of story elements, or the reason for the plot structure. As you continue to read, think aloud as you gather information that can help you infer the answer to your question.

2. Select another key strategy from the inventory of writing strategies in Chapter 7. Write a brief personal narrative that can be shared with friends, family, or students. Think aloud as you (a) select your topic, (b) organize information, (c) write a first draft, (d) make revisions, and (e) proofread. Record the processes you use.

3. Either select a problem that you have been confronted with and that you find challenging or use one of the following problems:
   ○ Resolve a checkbook balance that does not match your statement.
   ○ Figure out how to satisfy two commitments that require your attendance at the same time.
   ○ Solve a crossword puzzle that has stumped you, or figure out how to complete a jigsaw puzzle that has many pieces of exactly the same color.

4. Focus on one of the strategies you use while trying to solve the problem, and record what you do when you are being persistent, flexible, or thorough and accurate.

Remember that extrapolating a strategy from your own behavior may differ in some respects from the way someone else would articulate the same strategy. Our goal is not to arrive at the ultimate, perfect task analysis but rather to guide students in an exploration of the inner workings of a complex behavior that they find perplexing. If, in the process of that exploration, you or your students come upon new insights, clearer terminology, or a need for revision, you have succeeded in engaging learners in the construction of knowledge—knowledge that they will own.

5

SAMPLE LESSON PLANS FOR EXPLICIT MEDIATION

We now have the design and substance for providing explicit mediation. We have a research-based instructional plan for teaching a strategy, and we have analyzed and identified the components of the strategy we are teaching. This chapter will look at examples of lessons that create the context for explicitly mediating students' ability to make inferences.

As noted earlier, mediation consists of two contrasting teaching modalities. We begin with a teacher-directed lesson that introduces and models the use of a cognitive strategy. This is a generic lesson in that it is not content specific; it uses concrete materials or pictures. With some modifications, the lesson can be used with students in different grade levels. One could make a case for using the model lesson across the grades so that it serves as a reference point when coaching students to recall the process they have learned.

The lessons that follow the teacher-directed model provide opportunities to engage students in transactional mediation as they use the strategy to problem solve while reading, writing, and resolving questions. The lessons in Levels II, III, and IV are drawn from the larger units of study in which they are embedded. The subject matter of the lessons should be related to the essential questions and larger concepts being studied. This chapter's sample lessons are ones I have taught to intermediate elementary students, many of whom had difficulty answering inference questions. The lessons represent the experiences we want students to have at each level of instruction. The students' age, skills sets, and demonstrations of learning determine the level of support to be provided and the amount of time that should be spent at each level.

The following lessons are offered as examples, not as exemplars. Many of my graduate students have produced excellent alternatives and variations to these lessons, so I invite you to read critically and creatively. However, whether we are a novice or a seasoned teacher, when we stand in front of our students poised to try out a new approach or a bold new experiment, it is hard to avoid experiencing the discomfort of risk taking. The temptation is to reach for the security of a fully formed model. But ownership counts. Without ownership, energy goes out the window for teachers and students alike.

So to get over the jitters, I let my students in on my state of mind. I tell them we are on a maiden voyage that I believe will take us to the best possible way to become successful, lifelong learners. Students love that sense of adventure and the possibility of witnessing their all-knowing teacher in the act of learning.

Use the model lessons, especially the explicit teaching of the strategy, as you would a template for wood cutting or a dress pattern. Cut around the edges, but find your own rhythm, your own voice, your own choice of words.

Level I: Focus, Model, and Reflect

A. Focus

1. **Teacher tells students which strategy they are going to be taught.**
2. **Teacher clarifies the new concept.**
3. **Teacher explains or shows why the strategy is important and useful.**
4. **Teacher makes the connection between students' prior knowledge and the strategy.**

Teacher: I brought this object to class today (*hold an unusual, unfamiliar object for everyone to see*) to help me teach you about answering certain kinds of questions called inference questions. I have been noticing that those certain kinds of questions are giving you a hard time. I can tell because when I ask one of those questions, your faces show me that you are thinking hard, and your silence tells me that you are stumped.

I bet you can pick out the kind of question I'm talking about. Here are two questions about this object: (*Have the questions displayed.*)

- Question 1: What do you see when you look at this object carefully?
- Question 2: What do you think this object is used for?

Teacher: Which question is the inference question? Hint: it's the question that is harder to answer. Take two minutes to think about your answers. (*After waiting, continue.*) Turn to your partner and discuss your answers. When you are finished sharing your thoughts, we will talk about your answers with the whole group.

Students: (*They share answers and reactions to the questions.*)

Teacher: (*Summarize the discussion.*) You told me that you found the first question easier to answer because you just had to describe what you saw. The answers were right there. The second question was hard to answer because the answers were not right there. You did not know what the object is used for. You never saw it before. The second question is an inference question. (*Write the word inference on the board.*) We often get a signal in our heads and sometimes in our bodies when we have to make an inference. It's that "Oops, I don't know" feeling. It's actually a good thing. That feeling lets us know we may have to make an inference. It is not always a signal that you missed something or that you did something wrong. Raise your hand if you have ever been asked questions that gave you that feeling.

We're going to learn a strategy for making inferences today. We'll get some practice making inferences, and then we'll come back to this unusual object and answer the inference question "What do you think this object is used for?"

Actually, you already know a lot about making inferences. If you went out to meet your school bus in the morning and it did not come when it usually does, you could make the inference that the bus had a flat tire. What other inferences could you make?

Students: (*Possible responses*)

The driver was delayed.

There was a new driver who didn't know the route.

There was an accident, and the driver had to make a detour.

My clock was wrong, and I was too early or too late.

Teaching Points

- Give positive feedback to students for their ability to make inferences.
- Note the viability of inferences that are grounded in the reality of buses, drivers, weather, and road conditions as opposed to wild guesses.

B. Model

1. Teacher uses visual aids or manipulative materials to demonstrate how to use the strategy.

2. Teacher models think aloud, articulating the inference process.

Teacher: I'm going to show you how I make inferences to answer a question or solve a puzzle when I'm stumped. I want you to just watch and listen. When I'm finished, I'm going to ask you to tell me what you saw and heard.

I've been having a problem with garbage appearing on my lawn in the morning. I put my garbage cans out at night with the lids locked down, but when I go out in the morning to put the cans away, there is garbage all over my lawn, and it is not mine. So I collected some of that garbage. (*Hold up a clear plastic bag with garbage items.*) I need to make some inferences so that I can figure out where the garbage is coming from. Then I'll know which neighbors to talk to about the garbage, and I can ask them for their help in solving this annoying little problem. There are three possible sources of garbage. (*Sketch three houses and list the occupants below each—Mom, Dad, 7-year-old girl, etc.*)

Let me see what information I can gather from each piece of garbage. This is a crumpled-up piece of paper with lines on it—loose-leaf paper. There is no name on it, but the math examples written on it are just like the ones I did when I took high school geometry. We've got a crumpled-up paper plate. This is a receipt from Stop & Shop. The items on the receipt are Rice Krispies, milk, apples, shampoo, and Diet Coke. This is the wrapping for a Cheetah Girls CD. This is a sales slip from a girls' clothing store (*add the name of a local store*) for a pair of jeans.

(*When you finish examining all of the available information, think aloud about what the items have in common.*) Let's see if some of these things have some kind of connection that would lead me to their owner. The paper plate and the grocery receipt could belong to any of my neighbors. They are not much help. But some of these things do have something in common and could give me clues as to whose garbage this is. The geometry paper probably belonged to a 10th grader because that is the grade geometry is taught. The Cheetah Girls CD could belong to a young teenage boy or a girl. My 14-year-old granddaughter loves their music. The jeans receipt is from a store that only sells clothing for girls.

The geometry paper, the CD, and the jeans receipt have something in common. They probably belong to a teenager, and the music and the clothing store suggest it is a girl. I'm going to make the inference that this garbage is coming from the house across the street. Cindy Walker lives there. She is 15 years old and the only teenage girl living near my house. I'm going to make the inference that the garbage is coming from her family's garbage cans. I think the inference I made is pretty sound but I can't be positive, so when I speak to Cindy's parents, I'll tell them about the garbage problem and explain why I made the inference that it may be their garbage that ends up on my lawn.

C. Reflect

1. Teacher asks students to retell the steps of the process they observed and make a written record of the steps.

2. Teacher asks students to think-pair-share and write their answers to these questions:

a. What strategy are you learning?

b. Why are you learning it?

3. Students share their responses with the class and receive feedback from peers and teacher.

Teacher: Now I would like you to tell me what you saw and heard. (*Record the students' feedback, listing the following steps they observed.*)

1. There was something you wanted to know that was not stated.

2. You carefully gathered information that gave you clues so you could make inferences about what you want to know.

3. You also used information you knew from your own experience and from what you already know to make some inferences.

4. You looked for connections between all the pieces of information.

5. Then you made an inference about what you wanted to know that was supported by all the information you gathered. You eliminated guesses that were not supported by all the information.

6. You kept in mind that your inferences are guesses based on available information; they identify what is reasonably true.

Teaching Points

• If the students need prompting, repeat the things you said during the lesson.

• Remind students to focus on the *thoughts* you articulated, not your actions (e.g., *read, looked, wrote, looked up*).

• Reframe responses when they are too broad. For example, if a student says, "You looked at the garbage," respond by saying, "Specifically, how did I do that?"

• Recast and label thinking behaviors. For example, if a student says, "You looked at a geometry paper," recast to "Yes, I gathered information."

• It is important not to skip the reflection period or to summarize what the students have learned for them.

Share and Reflect

Tell students that they did a great job describing how we make inferences. Ask them to check in with themselves to see what they have "digested." Ask them to take time to think about what they have learned about this strategy and why they are learning it; then turn to a partner and discuss their answers to those questions. Have students write their responses in their journals and then share them with the whole group.

Teaching Points

• Use this activity to affirm or to clarify students' understanding of how and why we make inferences.

• Assure students they will be getting a lot of practice in this important strategy.

Level II: Practice Problem Solving with the Strategy Using Visual Aids or Concrete Materials

A. Whole Group Practice

1. Students practice the strategy with peer and teacher support.

2. Students share questions and reactions and receive feedback.

3. Students reflect on their learning.

Teacher: Let's work together to infer what this unusual object, which I showed you earlier, is used for. Now we have a strategy to follow. (*Read the list of steps aloud.*)

Student: Is it a weapon?

Teacher: So your inference is the object is a weapon? What did you see that makes you think that?

Student: I see something pointy. There is also something heavy like a rock.

Teacher: So you observed two details that support your inference. (*Wait.*)

Student: I don't know what the straw part is for. Now I'm not sure.

Teacher: What will your next step be?

Student: (*Looking at the strategy list*) I did gather information and think about what I already know, but I didn't use all the information, like the white thing that looks like a fishhook or the straw-brush part.

Teacher: So you would like to consider some other possibilities?

Student: I'd like to look at the list of all the parts I see. Then maybe I'll get some new ideas. Now I'm wondering if this is something that goes in the water.

Teacher: Let's all work with your new strategy.

Teaching Points

  • Coach students as they refer to the listed steps of the strategy and go through the process of making an inference to answer the question.

  • Observe students' application of the strategy.

  • Encourage students to verbalize the processes they are using and to listen to how fellow students are approaching the task.

  • Clarify the difference between descriptions and other more elaborative and subjective responses.

• Monitor pitfalls like jumping to conclusions without considering all of the available information.

• Monitor for making subjective inferences that are not grounded in observations.

• Reinforce the use of accurate terminology.

• Provide positive feedback for thoroughness.

• Praise risk taking.

Share and Reflect

After students have shared their inferences and given feedback to each other, tell students to journal independently so they can consolidate what they learned and formulate any questions they have about making inferences.

B. Cooperative Group Practice

1. Students practice the strategy in a small group with teacher coaching.

2. Groups share the outcomes of their work with the whole class, receive feedback, and reflect on the process.

Teacher: You are on your way to becoming inference experts. You know that when an answer to a question cannot be found using your eyes and your ears, you have to do some thinking. You know how to gather information that provides clues which will lead you to make an educated guess.

Making inferences is so important to understanding our experiences, I want to be sure you own that strategy and you can take it out and use it anytime you need it. Therefore, today I'm going to step back so you can work on making inferences with more independence.

We are going to be doing the work of anthropologists today. Anthropologists gather information from studying artifacts and pictures to find out how people lived in times past. Since we have been investigating how our history has shaped our present day lives, would you like to find out what schools were like in the early days of our country? Do you think those early schools shaped the way our schools are today?

We are going to examine pictures and artifacts from a pre-Civil War school house. By using the strategy you learned for making inferences, you will be able to build an understanding of what schools were like at that time. First, we'll have a demonstration of the way we will be working. I'd like four people to volunteer to be the demonstrators. (*Using the "fishbowl" technique, have the volunteers sit in the middle of the room. Arrange the rest of the class around the inner circle of four students.*) Those of you in the outer circle have a very important job to do. You will be observers and note takers so that you can give the people in the "fishbowl" feedback on how they worked together, what you thought about the inferences they made, and what they may have done differently. (*Display pictures of an early American schoolroom, 19th century schoolbooks, a quill and ink, slate, and a paddle. Provide the group with one photo or item. Review guidelines for cooperative work, information gathering, and reporting. After the group has used their observations to make inferences about 19th century schooling, invite the observers to respond. Arrange the class in cooperative groups and provide each group with a photo or artifact.*)

Share and Reflect

Have groups share and discuss the outcomes of their collaboration with the whole class. Encourage students to infer what their classroom reveals about the way they are being taught and to make comparisons with education in the 19th century.

Elicit descriptions of the processes students are using to make inferences, and note comparisons. As students reflect on how the use of the strategy helped them make inferences, provide feedback and assess students' thoughtfulness, use of prior knowledge, and ability to draw reasonable conclusions. Evaluate their readiness for independent practice.

Teaching Points

- Cooperative activities are most successful when the time allotment and the procedures are clearly defined and roles are assigned to the group members.
- Remember, thinking is not linear; it is a recursive process. A flexible use of strategies is an important part of the process of making meaning.
- We are not suggesting that students memorize the list of steps for the focus strategy. They will internalize the behaviors you have demonstrated by using them and talking about them.

- Develop raps, rhythms, and rhymes using the key words from the strategy to punch up the important elements of the strategy and to make it distinctive.
- Observe if students are applying the strategies they were taught and are thinking productively.
- Note if students are thorough, persistent, and systematic in their approach to a task.
- Use your observations for on-the-spot feedback and coaching.
- Encourage student-to-student coaching.
- Evaluate students' needs for continued practice in a group or their readiness to work independently with the strategy.
- Depending on the age and ability of your students, consider using the following activities in conjunction with content studies:
  - Infer ideas about a people's lifestyle from an article of clothing.
  - Infer an animal's habitat from its features.
  - Infer the culture and technology of a community from a time capsule that was (supposedly) unearthed.
  - Infer the interests of a child from his toy chest.
  - Examine a plant and infer the care it received.
  - Infer the values of a society by examining a coin.
  - Infer the difference between two historical periods from representative paintings.

C. Independent Practice

1. Students practice using the target strategy independently.

2. Students journal as they work and share their responses with the teacher and the class when they are finished with the task.

3. Students take time to reflect and evaluate what they have learned.

Teacher: Would you say that the cover of a book influences your book selections? How much information can you get from the title, illustration, and author?

Students: (*The class shares answers.*)

Teacher: I have a class set of a book that has been purchased by our school. I would like you to decide whether or not you would be interested in reading this book judging from its cover. A book cover contains a lot of information for a person who is accustomed to making inferences. You probably will want to make inferences regarding the genre of the book, the story characters, and even the story problem. (No peeking inside!)

Since you are going to be deciding for yourself, you will be working on your own. Use a double-entry journal to record your observations on one side of the page and the inferences that you make from those observations on the other side of the page.

Share and Reflect

Students share their decisions and the inferences on which they were based with the whole class. Take a count of the students who will be reading the book. Allow time for students to return to their journals to reflect on their competence and confidence when making inferences.

Level III: Apply Strategy to a Problem-Solving Task

A. Model and Reflect Application

1. The teacher models the application of the strategy to a reading, writing, or problem-solving task.

2. Students retell what they observed.

3. Students reflect on the process and share their responses.

Teaching Points

• Model how you apply the inference strategy to answering questions based on fiction or nonfiction text taken from the content of the curriculum.

• Start by choosing an inference question requiring an extended response that draws on two or more pieces of information. Even though extended responses require making more connections, an inference that hinges on one detail is subtler and may be more difficult to grasp initially.

Teacher: (*Referring to* Dear Mr. Henshaw *by Beverly Cleary* [1983]) During our literature circle yesterday, some of you wondered why Leigh is writing to Mr. Henshaw so often. Answering that question would help us understand the character better and perhaps teach us something about human nature. It is true, Beverly Cleary doesn't actually tell us that answer, so is it possible to answer that question?

Students: (*If students do not make the connection between the inference strategy and this problem, offer a prompt such as "Which strategy could we use to answer a question when the answer is not given?"*)

Teacher: I'm going to show you how I use the same inference strategy we practiced with the object, picture, and artifacts we examined the other day to answer the question about Leigh. This time I'll base my inference on what I've read. Watch and listen as I read aloud and think aloud to gather information that will give me clues to answer the inference question "Why does Leigh write to Mr. Henshaw so much?" When I'm finished, I'll ask you to tell me what you saw and heard.

Teaching Points

- Read aloud and think aloud to demonstrate your process.
- Model how you use your awareness of the organization of the text to decide where to start reading to locate the information you need.
- Stop reading when you find details that relate to the question you are trying to answer. Think aloud as you reason about the connection you are making.
- Model note taking by using key words as opposed to copying the whole text. (This strategy would be taught explicitly prior to the strategy lesson.)
- Model how you monitor your progress. Think aloud as you check to be sure you are staying focused on the information that answers the question.
- Record the information you have found. Semantic mapping can be used as an alternative note-taking strategy.

Teacher: (*Summarize your findings.*) I read that Leigh is new in his school and he has not made any friends. His mother is working, so he doesn't have anyone to talk to when he comes home. He hardly gets to see his father because he is a truck driver who is on the road a lot and his parents are divorced. I see a connection between these details: no friends, mother working, and father away. Even though Beverly Cleary doesn't actually say so, based on what I read, I would make the inference that Leigh writes to Mr. Henshaw a lot because he is lonely. Before we talk about Leigh's actions, I'd like you to tell me what you saw and heard me do.

Students: (*Students help each other reconstruct what they observed. They note the strategy for gathering and connecting information to make an inference when reading is the same as the strategy they used before to make inferences about objects and pictures.*)

Reflect and Share

Ask students to think about what they learned and why they are learning it. After a few minutes, invite them to share their thoughts with a partner and then write their responses in their journals.

B. Whole Group Application

1. Students work with teacher support in applying the strategy to content material.

2. Students reflect and share responses and questions.

Teacher: I read through the journal notes you made during reading workshop yesterday and highlighted the questions that occurred to you. As you are sharing your questions with the rest of the class, we will try to figure out the answers together. If your question stumps all of us, I'll write it on the board.

Students: (*The class shares and responds to questions as a group.*)

Teacher: We are going to select one question we had trouble answering, and we'll tackle it together. Since we are going to be on a hunt for clues that can help us answer the question, why don't you select a strategy for recording the information that you find? (*Students can use highlighting tape, note taking, a semantic map, or sticky notes.*)

Teaching Points

• Working in a whole group, coach students as they reread to gather information and make inferences to answer their questions.

• Coach students in the use of other key strategies, as needed, while reading.

- Students can take turns reading aloud, stopping when the text relates to the question, and explaining the inference they are making from the information.
- Students can monitor each other, interjecting when they think pertinent information has been left out or when irrelevant information has been selected.
- Using the notes that have been recorded on the board, guide students in the construction of a well-developed written response to the question.

Share and Reflect

Give students feedback on their progress in making thoughtful inferences when reading. Make them aware that the answer they developed meets the criteria for a top score on the reading and writing assessments because of its thoroughness, accuracy, clarity, and well-supported conclusions. Use these criteria to develop a rubric for students to use for self-assessment when giving other extended responses.

Discuss any pitfalls that you observed. Ask students to reflect on their comfort with answering questions that are based on information that is not directly stated. Compare how it feels to answer an inference question now with how it used to feel.

C. Cooperative Group Application

1. Students apply the strategy to content material with teacher coaching.

2. Groups share the outcome of their work with the whole class, receive feedback and reflect on their processes.

Teacher: Do you think you are ready to do some detective work with your buddies? Now that we have finished reading Beverly Cleary's *Dear Mr. Henshaw*, I have a question for you to ponder. (*Write the question on the board.*) Leigh Botts, the main character in *Dear Mr. Henshaw*, was faced with several problems in this book. You can refer back to the page in your journal where you drew a web and recorded the main story line and all the subplots or problems Leigh had to resolve. Here is my question: Do you think writing to Mr. Henshaw helped Leigh overcome his problems? Find examples from the book to support your answer. (*Engage students in planning their strategies for answering this question.*) It will be very interesting to see if the inferences you make to answer this question will be similar or different.

Teaching Points

- While students are working cooperatively, observe the initiation of strategies that support a thorough review of the text.
- Note if students are monitoring their work and adjusting their strategies to meet the demands of the task.
- Coach students who are having difficulty using literal information to draw inferences.
- Note which parts of the process are challenging and need further support.
- Note if answers are well supported with information in the text.

Share and Reflect

Each cooperative group shares their answer and explains the process they used. Pitfalls such as a lack of thoroughness and unsupported guesses should be pointed out and alternative strategies suggested. Discuss and debate the differences in the inferences that were made. Draw conclusions about positive ways we can solve serious problems in our lives. Emphasize how much we enhance our understanding when we make inferences.

D. Independent Application

1. **Students apply the strategy working without peer or teacher coaching.**
2. **Students share the outcome of their work with the whole class, receive feedback, and reflect on what they learned and the process they used.**

Teacher: The information you will be reading provides details about an early American homestead. When you have finished reading the portion of the text that describes the homestead, stop reading. Using the details in the text and the inferences you make, draw a picture of how you visualize what a homestead looked like.

Teaching Points

- Prepare your visualization while the students are creating theirs.
- Use this product of your students' understanding to assess the degree to which inferential thinking has become a part of their reading process.

- Evaluate the thoroughness and plausibility of the inferences made.
- Note the students' ease or reluctance when they are asked to make inferences.
- Encourage reflection and discussion of the other strategies students used to accomplish the task.

Teacher: Place your drawings and writings around the room. Let's take time to observe and compare what each of us has inferred from our reading. (*After a substantial wait, ask students to share what they know from what they read as opposed to what they inferred. Use the information they have gathered to build declarative knowledge. Raise questions and make inferences concerning the larger issues that relate to homesteaders in 19th century America, such as the quality of life, dangers, advantages, reasons for becoming homesteaders, what role these people played in the history of this country, and how the actions of the homesteaders affect the lives we live today.*)

Share and Reflect

Invite students to raise questions and share reactions to the activity. Ask students to consider how their understanding of what they read was affected by the inferences they made. Ask if the activity made remembering the material easier and, if it did, why that was so. Check in with students to find out what other strategies they used to clarify and remember what they read. Guide the observation of the likenesses and differences in students' thinking. Ask if there is anything they heard from their classmates that they intend to add to their repertoire of strategies.

Level IV: Transfer Strategy to Problem-Solving Tasks

A. Model and Reflect on Transfer of the Strategy

1. Teacher models the application of the focus strategy in different contexts across the curriculum and in problem-solving situations.

2. Students retell what they observed.

3. Students think-pair-share-write their answers to these questions:
   a. **What did you learn?**
   b. **Why are you learning it?**

Teacher: I want to share a little story with you. Last weekend it rained very hard. You may remember that. It was quite a storm. I was visiting a neighbor during that storm. Well, while we were sitting and talking in the living room, we started to hear a plunking sound. We followed the sound, and it led to the bedroom. There in the middle of the room was a large puddle of water. Above the puddle was a soggy hole in the ceiling.

If we didn't do something, my neighbor was going to have a pond in his bedroom. The wood floor was getting soaked, and you know what happens to wood when it gets wet? It swells and splits and cracks. I said, "Let's get a big container and put it under the drip to protect the floor while we are trying to fix the leak." My neighbor said, "I don't have a big container I can use for this drip." I said I would see what I could find.

When I walked into the bathroom and looked under the sink, there was a nice big plastic bucket. I brought the bucket to my neighbor and said, "What about this?" My neighbor said, "That bucket is for cleaning the bathroom." My neighbor didn't realize that he could take something that is useful in one place and use it in another place. We don't want to make the same mistake as my neighbor—who now has ducks living in his bedroom. Just kidding!

Today I'm going to show you how we can take the strategies we are using when we read and write and use them when we need them in another kind of situation.

Teaching Points

• The strategies that students learn to solve problems should flow outward and lead to a larger sense of how to solve problems in the world they inhabit.

• Students have limitless opportunities to transfer the use of key strategies while engaged in classroom activities, social interactions, personal decision making, civic responsibilities, event planning, and problem solving.

Teacher: Every year each classroom in our school is given a budget of $300 to purchase materials, books, or supplies. I would like your help in selecting the items we order for our class. Before I hand out the catalogs, I want you to listen and watch as I show you the process I use when selecting the items.

I want to choose wisely. When I'm ordering an item I haven't used before, there is a risk I may be disappointed when it arrives. The quality may be poor, and I'll end up wasting the money. Ordering from a catalog is really guesswork. All I can do is read the descriptions and make an educated guess based on what the catalogue tells me. Wait a minute—making an educated guess based on information is what I do when I make inferences. I'm pretty good at making inferences. I know enough to gather all the information and not jump to conclusions. I know how to use my previous experiences and the new information to make judgments and arrive at conclusions. (*Select an item in the catalog, read the copy, look at the picture, check the measurements against a ruler, and relate information to prior knowledge. Collect details that either support or reject the purchase of the item.*) Now tell me what you heard and saw.

Students: (*Ask students to retell the steps they used in this new task.*)

Teacher: Think about three times you make inferences today. After a few minutes, turn to your partner and share the situations you encountered that required inferential thinking. When you think you have gotten to the answer you want to give, write it in your journals and answer the following questions: What did you learn? Why are you learning it?

Teaching Point

• Assess students' awareness of the importance of making well-grounded inferences when making decisions and formulating ideas in response to situations they encounter.

B. Whole Group Transfer

1. The teacher prompts students to engage in the selection of task-appropriate strategies while working in subjects across the curriculum and in nonacademic problem-solving situations.

2. Students journal, reflect, and share their processes to maintain metacognitive dialogue and learn from each other.

Teacher: Let's continue to choose items to order within our $300 budget. Starting in cooperative groups, examine the items in the catalog you have. Select the ones you are in favor of ordering. Then when each group is ready, we will have each spokesperson take a turn and read the description of the item you picked. We'll work together to infer the quality and practicality of buying the items you selected.

Share and Reflect

After the groups have shared the choices they made and the reasons for their selections, ask them to journal about whether knowing how we make inferences gave them more confidence in their decision making.

C. Cooperative Group Transfer

1. Students select appropriate strategies to complete tasks from across the curriculum while working cooperatively.

2. Students share their processes and products with the whole group, receive feedback, and reflect on the outcome of their efforts.

Teacher: You have decided you want to investigate the effectiveness of hand sanitizers in preventing illness. As you work with your group, you will be following the protocol for the scientific method for this investigation. That means we will follow these steps:

1. Gather your observations and form a hypothesis about the effects of the use of sanitizers while in school.
2. Design an experiment to test your predictions.
3. Collect the data from your experiment.
4. Examine the results of the experiment in light of your original hypothesis.
5. Draw your conclusions.
6. Construct a graphic representation of your experiment results.

Teaching Point

• The scientific method provides many opportunities to apply the strategies for making sound inferences. Remind students to examine their conclusions for faulty logic, weak premises, insufficient connections, and the use of misinformation.

Share and Reflect

Ask students to share their conclusions from their studies using charts and graphs with the class. Have students suggest ways to disseminate their study results to other classrooms in the school and to the community.

With your students, develop standards for evaluating conclusions that can be applied to studies, reports, editorials, and claims made in various sources of information. Those standards can be used to develop a rubric for making and evaluating conclusions.

D. Independent Transfer

1. Students regulate, monitor, and evaluate their reading, writing, and problem solving by selecting task-appropriate strategies when working in content areas and when problem solving.

2. Students maintain process journals, construct rubrics, and receive peer and teacher feedback to evaluate and revise works in progress.

Teaching Points

• Once students demonstrate their ownership of a strategy, prompt students to apply and transfer behaviors they have learned in different contexts.

• Assess students' ability and willingness to persist when problem solving. Note their resourcefulness and flexibility in selecting appropriate strategies.

• Provide students with ongoing opportunities to teach and explain the use of strategies to others.

• Students assess their own learning and achievement by maintaining process journals, creating personalized rubrics, and monitoring their own behaviors and progress.

Summary

Before we move on to investigate the other key strategies we will want to teach (see chapters 6, 7, and 8), let me summarize the trajectory of putting explicit transactional strategy mediation into action. We start by watching our students. We observe and assess which of our students' behaviors prevent them from reading with understanding, writing with clarity, and solving problems effectively.

Knowing that strategy mediation is an ongoing process and we will want to allocate time to each of the key strategies, we would prioritize mediation based on what we have observed and select a strategy that will, in effect, "give us the biggest bang for the buck." We prepare for instruction by analyzing the strategy so that we have a step by step guide for our model lesson. With map in hand, we begin an explicit conversation with our students so that they understand how they will benefit from the journey we are taking them on.

Next, we survey our curriculum and decide where we want to embed our strategy lessons. We select lessons which will provide opportunities for our students to problem solve and will provide opportunities for us to engage in coaching transactions with them. We plan for an extended period of scaffolded instruction that will allow our students to grow their expertise by practicing and applying the new strategy in varied contexts.

Using our students' transactions, conferences, reflections, discussions, and work products, we make decisions about: the pace of our lessons, the differentiation of instruction, when to release control, and when to introduce a new focus strategy. Throughout this orchestral process, we maintain a balance between teaching process and product, learner and learning.

6

LOOKING UNDER THE HOOD:
KEY READING STRATEGIES

The first time I had to put a quart of oil in my two-tone blue Ford Maverick, I lifted the car's hood and was appropriately dismayed and intimidated. The collage of metal, plastic, and rubber was unintelligible to me. It was impossible to differentiate or identify the tightly packed maze of parts. That mystifying experience comes to mind when I think about the complex nature of the work teachers must do when they assess their students' abilities and difficulties. Like mechanics who are able to identify car troubles by looking under the hood, teachers must be able to distinguish and label what they are seeing when they observe their students in action so they can spot malfunction and set about fixing it. Knowing what you are looking at is paramount to getting the job done.

The complexity of assessing our students is compounded by the existence, in the literature, of different frameworks, labels, and lenses with which to classify and identify reading, writing, and thinking behaviors. So the first aim of this chapter is to define the strategies we mediate and go beyond the abstract labels to look at the anatomy of each essential strategy—its facets, its cognitive requirements, and its impact on proficiency. The exploration of the strategies addressed in this chapter is intended to dispel common misconceptions, enhance understanding, and facilitate the process of task analysis.

The second focus of this chapter is to suggest ways to use student demonstrations in the classroom for ongoing formative assessment. What are the glitches in those performances that interfere with students' ability to experience success? What strategies do students need to learn in order to repair the glitches?

Key Reading Strategies

We can identify the core reading strategies by thinking about our own thinking as we read. Therefore, before reading on, I encourage you to settle into a comfortable chair with a good book and proceed to read aloud and think aloud. When you have read a few pages, stop and review your thoughts. Then label them.

For example, these are the responses I had as I began to read Tobias Wolff's (1989) memoir *This Boy's Life* (pp. 3, 4). The labels for each of my thoughts and reactions are in parentheses:

I have wanted to read this memoir. This title has come up several times in talking about the memoir I'm writing. I'm told it's a modern classic and a great example of how a memoir uses information for illumination and transcends the lives of the people in it. On another level I want to pay attention to how Wolff writes about the past in real time so it reads like a novel. I would like to be able to do that with my writing. (*Activating schema—text-to-self connection*)

Oh, I see it got the PEN/Faulkner Award. That's not easy to do. I'm going to try to identify the qualities that made this an award winning book. (*Activating prior knowledge—text-to-text connection*)

The title is stirring a very early memory of some book or magazine my brother had back when he was in elementary school in the late 1940s or early '50s. Oh, the copyright page has Wolff's date of birth—1945. He's a few years younger than my brother. I will probably be able to relate to the era this book is set in. (*Activating prior knowledge—text-to-self; inferring*)

The lead is like a carry-on bag, so short, simple, and loaded with important stuff—a boy and his mother, a car that keeps boiling over, and the Continental Divide. Taking to the road in a wreck has me thinking these people are up against it and there is some urgency about their trip. (*Inferring; synthesizing*)

The Continental Divide. That has to be one of the most majestic settings I've ever experienced. Those magnificent mountains, towering conifers, walking on frozen ice-blue glacial water knowing you're at a unique place where three of the world's oceans converge. I wonder if that setting is biographically accurate or if Wolff placed the characters there because it is a metaphor for a choice of directions, a split. Where would they be headed to? (*Activating prior knowledge—text-to-self; visualizing; questioning*)

The next sentence just sneaks up on you the way the next event sneaks up on the boy and his mom. Wolff tells us they're waiting for the engine to cool and there's the "bawling of an air horn." Before you can digest what you read, you realize if the car hadn't boiled over, the runaway truck would have smashed them into oblivion. (*Inferring*)

The imagery is handled so subtly and powerfully. The sound and the fury of the massive, out-of-control machine followed by the sigh of the wind in the trees and the truck lying upturned on the boulders in the river below the cliff, looking pitifully small. . . . The fragility of life really registers with this scene. (*Visualizing; interpreting*)

The way Toby's mother reaches out to touch her son makes me think she's feeling the fragility of life. Just her gesture speaks volumes—her sensitivity, the strength of their relationship, their vulnerability. I have a feeling the mother and son are in for a harrowing time. Perhaps there will be separate or parallel narratives that sustain each other in some way. (*Predicting; inferring; making judgments; determining important ideas*)

So Wolff shows us Toby's hand for the first time. He overrides his mother's emotions in the aftermath of the tragedy and her lack of funds to make a play for souvenirs. He's quite the manipulator. There's a level of detachment in him that's kind of unsettling. (*Inferring; making judgments*)

So I found out that Toby and his mother are running away from her abusive boyfriend. They are going to try to get rich on uranium in Utah. This strong mother and her willful son may be the stuff of a tale of survival and redemption. I'm hooked. (*Retelling; synthesizing; inferring; reacting*)

I thought I would be able to relate to this story that is set in 1950s. We may have lived in the same era, but the external similarities end there. (*Adjusting predictions; activating prior knowledge—text-to-self connection*)

Compare the list that emerged from my reading and yours with the following summary of the cognitive behaviors identified in both the proficient reader studies of the 1980s and the subsequent research cited by the National Reading Panel (National Institute of Child Health and Human Development, 2000) that identified the essential strategies that interactive, meaning-making readers consistently use:

• Activating and making connections with relevant prior knowledge (schema) before, during, and after reading text.
• Drawing inferences from the text in the form of predictions, conclusions, judgments, interpretations, hypotheses, and envisionments.
• Summarizing or organizing text while reading to determine text structure and message.
• Asking questions of themselves, the author, and the text to clarify and focus reading.
• Monitoring understanding, adjusting rate and analytic behavior depending on the demands of the text, and employing fix-up strategies to maintain meaning and repair comprehension.
• Synthesizing text and reflecting on what the big ideas in the text are. (p. 15)

Paradoxically, although these strategies are used by highly literate readers, they also define basic and essential reading behaviors. In addition, by thinking aloud, you notice that you do not use these strategies in any particular order; you cannot place them in a hierarchy. Our reading demonstrates that proficient readers use multiple strategies recursively when interacting with the text. The interplay of strategies that enables you to construct meaning as you read makes prioritizing the strategies impossible. If you were to eliminate any one strategy, your ability to make meaning would be at the very least diminished, if not lost. So even though each key strategy will be discussed individually and initially taught separately and directly, explicit mediation of students' reading will foster the use of the full range of strategies when constructing meaning and problem solving.

The spontaneous use of these strategies or cognitive behaviors can easily lull us into the assumption that our responses to text are inherent to all readers. However, that is not always the case for a variety of reasons, ranging from a lack of exposure to printed language to language-processing problems. When students demonstrate minimal or superficial comprehension and recall, we can intervene and teach them to engage in the use of the full range of proficient reader strategies.

The conclusion of the National Reading Panel (National Institute of Child Health and Human Development, 2000) in regard to instruction that enhances comprehension is an apt introduction to our study of key reading strategies:

> The rationale for the explicit teaching of comprehension skills is that comprehension can be improved by teaching students to use specific cognitive strategies or to reason strategically when they encounter barriers to understanding what they are reading. Readers acquire these strategies informally to some extent, but explicit or formal instruction in the application of comprehension strategies has been shown to be highly effective in enhancing understanding. The teacher generally demonstrates such strategies for students until the students are able to carry them out independently. (p. 14)

Pearson and Duke (2002) point out, "Comprehension improves when teachers provide explicit instruction of the use of comprehension strategies. Comprehension improves when teachers implement activities that support the understanding of the text that students will read in their classes" (p. 247).

Although more attention has been paid to the instructional development of reading skills in weaker readers than in average and above-average readers, there are many high school and college readers whose comprehension is disappointing, so there is good reason to address the comprehension of those who are among the best readers in our schools as well (Pressley, 2001).

Activating Relevant Prior Knowledge (Schema) Before, During, and After Reading Text

Well before I knew what I know now about teaching strategies, I knew that cumbersome teacher-directed, prereading lessons that resulted in covering three wall boards with tentacled brainstorming maps or snaking lists of topic-related vocabulary was not the way to change my students' activation of prior knowledge. Unless I were going to be propped like Jiminy Cricket on each of my student's shoulders before, during, and after reading, I would have to give them some tools they could carry with them and use independently.

Strategy Anatomy

Schema theory proposes that knowledge is stored within organizational systems in the brain. These "files" are sometimes called the building blocks of cognition. To appreciate how activating the "files" that are relevant to what we read impacts our understanding and learning, we have only to think about what we already know (our schema) about activating prior knowledge and experience. For example, based on what you know, how would you prefer to approach an interview for a teaching position? Would you like to walk in "cold," or would you prefer to prepare yourself by thinking about the kinds of information and issues that would be relevant in a conversation with school administrators, supervisors, and teachers?

You know that such preparation would give you the opportunity to organize your thoughts, think about what information you need to gather in advance, and create a framework of expectations against which you can monitor your performance. You would have increased confidence during the interview because you would be prepared to ask questions and give substantive responses supported by relevant details. You would know which of your experiences and skills should be brought to the table. You would be able to communicate more effectively if, for example, you knew your interviewer's cognitive style and were prepared to make accommodations such as presenting ideas in a logical-sequential or a random-subjective way.

Our own positive experiences with activating prior knowledge are reflected in reading research that has shown conclusively and repeatedly that when readers draw on their own experience and schema, comprehension improves (Pressley et al., 1992). We can expand our students' awareness of the many ways to think about text before, during, and after reading. Some of those ways help them process and understand content. Other ways of thinking about the text engage students by raising questions they want to answer and fostering predictions they will want to confirm or reject. Confidence, interest, questions, and predictions increase the level of attention students invest in their reading. Attending is the linchpin of comprehension. When learners are actively processing what they read, the neuronal networks in which information and concepts are encoded actually increase in size and complexity, thereby adding to the pathways for long-term memory (Lowery, 2001; Wolfe, 2001).

What questions do we want students to ask themselves in order to activate prior knowledge and experience? Each of the questions listed here can be explored in the context of explicit transactional instruction. They frame multilayered conversations that require thoughtful, problem-solving discussions of schema:

• How can I infer the topic of the book? What do I know about this topic? Are there prominent words or geographic locations that I need to look up before I start reading?

• How can I identify the genre of this book? What do I know about that genre that will tell me what kind of writing to expect? What predictions can I make based on what I know about the genre? Does this remind me of other books I've read? Why?

• Who is the author? What other books have I read by this author? What do I know, like, or dislike about the author's style, clarity, difficulty, veracity, and complexity?

• How is the text organized? Will I need to take notes or map the information for the task I have to do? What pace of reading is suitable for this kind of reading?

• Before and during reading: Is this book triggering my own personal memories? Are the characters' or author's perspective giving me cause to re-examine my own perspective? Are my expectations and predictions accurate?

• After reading: Did reading this book change what I think about the topic, the ideas, or the author? What were those changes?

Formative Assessment of Strategies

To gather the information we need to determine what kinds of support students require, we must be sure to look in the right places. Regie Routman (1996) describes the climate for assessment that serves our needs:

[E]valuation is not a separate piece or an end in itself. I now know it is part of reading and writing and everything we do in our classrooms and beyond, it is ongoing, on-the-spot, integral to our instructional effectiveness every day. We are constantly evaluating and re-evaluating what we do, where we and our students are in our learning processes, and continually setting and resetting goals. (p. 149)

While standardized and norm-referenced testing will continue to be a fact of life in classrooms everywhere, the only way to assess students' procedural knowledge is by observing processes—how students read, write, and solve problems. Collecting answers and looking for errors does not give us the information we need to determine where those processes are breaking down and what transactional instruction is needed.

The information we need to make the learning and learner match is available to us every minute of every day in our classrooms. Teachers are walking databases. The information we gather determines how we grade, teach, discipline, organize our rooms, and interact with our students. Formative assessment is an extension of the kind of watching that we do. Although assessment is not a major focus of this book, I would like to highlight some of the classroom activities that allow us to gather the information we need to identify our students' challenges and differentiate their mediation. The activities listed here require students to process information; that is, they enrich students' examination and elaboration of the text. They are not contrived exercises done for the explicit purpose of providing the teacher with ways to catch what students do not know.

Activities for Assessing Students' Ability to Activate Relevant Prior Knowledge

We can gather information for making formative assessments from the following activities:

- Read-alouds and think-alouds
- Double-entry journals
- Student-teacher conferences

- Book discussions or literary circles
- Graphic organizers

Demonstrations of Students' Ability to Activate Relevant Prior Knowledge

To determine whether students are purposefully activating schema and benefiting from the use of that strategy, I want to know if my students are

- Identifying the genre, title, organizational structure, typographical cues, chapter headings, and lead sentences.
- Inferring the content of the text prior to reading from the title, genre, illustrations, chapter headings, and skimming.
- Recalling personal experiences related to the text.
- Questioning and comparing information that differs from their prior knowledge.
- Noting that the text has affected their previous understanding or point of view.
- Comparing the author or book to other authors or books.
- Using what they already know about the organization of the material to make predictions.
- Using what they know about the genre of the text to make predictions.
- Using their prior knowledge of the subject to make judgments and criticisms about the text's accuracy and realism.
- Using prior experience to create sensory images that enhance the text's meaning.
- Engaging in their reading as a result of making meaningful personal connections.

Drawing Inferences: Eric and Trent

I came to expect the comradery and enthusiasm that encircled my eight 5th graders when we gathered around the large rectangular conference table in the reading room. They enjoyed the kind of familiarity that is usually reserved for siblings or bunk mates at sleepaway camp by the end of summer. I had been meeting with most of the children in the group since the time they were struggling beginning readers.

These students were all loveable in their own right, but they occupied a special place in my heart because they had traveled with me through the uncharted course of explicit strategy instruction. It was their bright eyes and eager responses that spurred me on and showed me what was possible.

I had taken a backseat in their discussion of Katherine Paterson's *The Great Gilly Hopkins* and was basking in the beauty of their self-guided exploration of the text when suddenly things got testy. Trent, the picture of confident coolness with his gelled hair, designer clothes, and a dimpled smile that was already garnering him popularity with the girls, was putting down Eric's comments. "No, she's not. You don't know what you're talking about. Miss Harris is trying to make Gilly mad so she'll get in more trouble."

Whatever qualities kids would ascribe to being cool, it is safe to say Eric did not possess them. He was sensitive, soft-spoken, shy, normally lacking in confidence, and a long way off from discovering hair gel. That's why my heart started to race when he looked Trent squarely in his eyes and said with steady certainty, "That's my inference, and I am entitled to make it!"

Could Eric have taken that stand if he hadn't learned that an inference is an educated guess based on available information and prior experience? Would Eric have challenged Trent's certainty if he did not know that people may draw different inferences that are equally valid? Without that understanding, would Eric have been empowered, in that moment of conflict, to be uncommonly assertive? I truly believe the answer to those questions is no.

Strategy Anatomy

Our observations make it clear that making inferences is pervasive to human activity and human survival. Frequently, the catalyst for making any inference is a perceived gap in information or understanding on the part of a viewer, listener, thinker, or reader. It is an innate function of the brain to make meaning (Caine & Caine, 1991). We automatically try to fill in the gaps that occur in our thinking and understanding. By using given data and prior knowledge, we fill in those gaps and either arrive at logical conclusions or make judgments

(Marzano, 2007). In effect, it is as if we are taking a leap from the known to the unknown. Inferring is a knowledge-producing or generative thinking behavior that we use each time we make predictions, generalize, draw conclusions, make judgments, surmise themes, interpret figurative language, derive word meaning from context, envision, and formulate hypotheses (see Figure 6.1). By making inferences when reading, we are able to maintain meaning, construct knowledge, and deepen personal enjoyment.

I did not always know the folly of "teaching" how to make inferences by giving my students a brief selection or a still briefer paragraph followed by a question and a choice of four answers. When it dawned on me, it hit me hard: "What does this have to do with becoming a more thoughtful reader? When

Figure 6.1 | **Inferential Thinking**

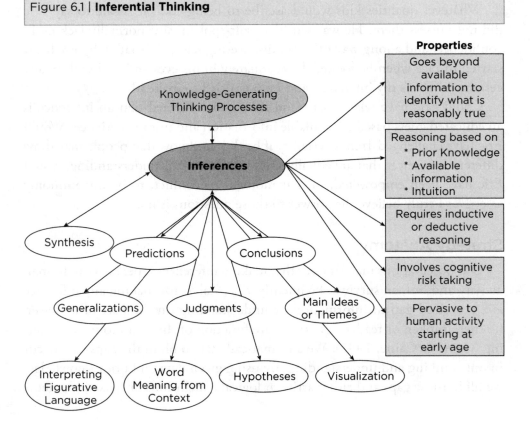

was the last time someone gave me a multiple-choice example to complete when I was reading a book?"

Question: When is the only time to give students multiple-choice exercises with inference questions?

Answer: When you want to give students practice in answering inference questions in multiple-choice exercises.

Contrary to what I've heard over the years, inferences are not a higher level of thinking that should be reserved for older or smarter kids. If you have ever heard a 5-year-old say to his mother, "You love Tommy better than me," you were hearing a young child make an inference, albeit perhaps a shaky one. My lower-achieving students engage in book conversations chock-full of inferences of all kinds, such as predictions, analysis, definitions of words from context, hypotheses, judgments, envisionments, and conclusions. Mental dispositions, such as attention to detail, precise processing, persistence, and flexibility, are frequently responsible for inadequate inferential thinking.

I had to wonder, if inferential thinking is a cognitive function pervasive to human activity, why did I find that, across the grades, students' scores on test items that required inferential thinking were consistently lower than their scores on test items that required literal thinking? Why did teachers consistently complain that students frequently answer, "It doesn't say," when they are asked an inference question? If those test results and that response are accurate indicators of our students' use of inferential thinking when they read, we may reasonably suspect they are missing the richest part of the reading experience.

When we take a closer look at this conundrum, we can make some clarifying distinctions. Inferential thinking often breaks down when students (1) do not recognize they are being asked an inference question and assume the answer is supposed to be found in their memory, (2) are required to explain unstated ideas in the text that had not occurred to them while reading, (3) are working too little or too hard on processing text, and (4) are not willing to engage in risk taking. These obstacles to inferential thinking can be addressed in the following ways:

• Working within the framework of explicit transactional mediation, teach students, starting in the primary grades, to recognize an inference question when they meet one. I use a drawing of a three-story house to teach the differences among questions that require literal, inferential, and creative responses (Costa, 2001b). This drawing is a place to hang my little talk about "right there" answers, "search and find" answers, and "on your own" answers. The practice in recognizing and answering the three different kinds of questions takes place in the context of literature discussions and content-area research.

• Preface inference questions with the words, "What do you think." Listen to the difference:

  ○ Why did Dr. De Soto decide to help the fox?
  ○ Why do you think Dr. De Soto decided to help the fox?

We send a confusing message when we ask an inference question in a way that suggests there is only one acceptable answer. Students who are short on confidence and fearful of being "wrong" will almost always do poorly with these questions unless we raise their awareness, take the mystery out of making inferences, provide encouragement, and give positive feedback. A good instructional plan will not do the trick without shoring up the affective side of making inferences.

• Inferring answers to someone else's questions is much more challenging than making inferences that spring from the comfort zone of our own thought processes. When students are cognizant of how literal questions differ from inference questions and are still unable to arrive at an inference that is anchored in the text, we need to take the next step and provide explicit mediation that breaks down and clarifies that strategy.

• Higher-order thinking has a dialectical relationship with the literal level of the text in the same way flowers relate back to the seeds in the soil and the seeds relate back to the flowers. To infer, analyze, judge, compare, and synthesize, we have to understand the text at the literal level. If students are working too hard at maintaining fluency they will not have much or any energy left over for higher-order responses to their reading. For that reason, I am fond of beginning book discussions with students taking turns retelling segments of the story they read. It is an opportunity to clarify the text at the literal level before going on to ponder interpretive questions.

• If students are not engaged when they read, if they are skipping over the surface of the page like a Frisbee skimming a lawn, they will not have the grist for the higher-order processing mill. Because students do not relish getting down to the bottom of the page or the end of the story without being able to remember what they have read, they will sign on for some practical solutions to their attention problems. Reading with pencil in hand changes the dynamic of superficial word calling; if a reader is not making meanings, she becomes aware of that fact because she has nothing to write. Here are some reading responses that students can use effectively while reading with a buddy or reading independently:

- Taking notes
- Using graphic organizers
- Journaling
- Drawing what is visualized
- Writing a question before turning each page

Activities for Assessing Students' Ability to Make Inferences

- Read-aloud/think-aloud
- Visualization and drawing
- Dramatization
- Double-entry journals
- Literary circle discussions
- Students' questions
- Open-ended or global questions
- Interpretive questions
- Student-teacher conferences
- Cooperative learning projects

Demonstrations of Students' Ability to Make Inferences

Because inferential thinking occurs on the input, processing, and output levels of information processing, our classrooms provide a veritable laboratory for data that enable us to assess our students' inferencing ability and identify the students who need mediation. We want to know if students are

- Bringing their original conclusions, predictions, and judgments to book discussions.

- Using the title, author, genre, and text organization to make predictions prior to reading and guessing the outcome of a selection after reading a portion of the text.
- Using context clues to infer the meaning of unfamiliar words.
- Getting meaning from the author's use of figurative language.
- Making inferences to resolve ambiguities or perplexities in the text.
- Using details to envision the appearance of characters and settings.
- Using details and narration to infer characters traits, behaviors, and reactions not stated in the text.
- Using narration and dialogue to hypothesize about the characters' motives.
- Using the narration and story events to infer the author's point of view.
- Using stated information to construct hypothetical events, dialogue, or outcomes.
- Guessing what action or incident might have taken place between two explicitly stated actions or incidents.
- Providing the main idea, general significance, theme, or moral that is not explicitly stated in the text.

Summarizing

In 4th grade, Keena was a fluent and expressive reader, but she could not retell or discuss the material she had just finished reading unless she reread the text or referred to her notes. Her note taking reflected her inability to tell the forest from the trees. It was no wonder her recall was so poor—her densely packed journal pages demonstrated that she was not differentiating or organizing the text.

Figure 6.2 shares two entries from Keena's reading journal. The first one was written at the beginning of the 4th grade. The second entry was written after weeks of mediation.

Strategy Anatomy

What is the remedy for clutter and confusion? Organization, of course. What is good for our closets happens to be good for our brains as well. To understand and remember, we have to put things together that go together in some way.

Figure 6.2 | **Two Entries from a Student's Reading Journal:
Before and After Mediation for Summarizing**

Before Mediation

Keena   November 4th
Writing   Mrs. Koenig

Dear Mr. Henshaw

Mom said she couldn't work and look after a
dog. It's easier to stay awake on long hauls
if he has someone to talk to. The dog
would be bored since Leigh and his mother
are gone so much. Bandit likes to ride and
that's how they got him. He jumped into
daddy's car at a truckstop in Nevada and
sat there. They called him Bandit because
he had a bandana on and not a collar.
Leigh lies in bed and thinks about Dad and
Bandit, because he hears a ping-pinging sound
from the gas station. He is glad because
Bandit is with dad keeping him awake.
Interstate 5 is a straight and boring with
nothing much but cotton fields and a big feed
lot that you can smell a long way before
you come to it. Mommy said not to worry
about the postage, so I can't use that
as an excuse for not answering. Leigh will
never write questions to an author even if

Figure 6.2 | **(Continued)**

After Mediation

(pages 46–53)

Chunking

1) Got phone call from dad.

2) He hoped he liked the jacket.

3) He wished his father lived with him.

4) His lunch was safe again.

5) His name did not work, his cake was missing.

6) He put scotch tape on his lunchbox.

7) Asks his mother a lot of questions.

Questions

1) Why do they put it on a tray?

2) Why does he say look out?

3) What is false teeth?

4) Why do they say tip all over your lip? He is sad. ☹

5) Why did he say put a burgular alarm? (Mr. Fridley)

6) How could anybody put a burgular alarm on a paper bag?

When we read, we count on written language to be organized. Our job is to either recognize or infer what the "glue" is that holds the sentences together. That is the act of summarizing. Feuerstein (1980) speaks to this fundamental cognitive process: "Summative behavior represents a basic need to produce relationships in the world, and it represents the active contribution of the organism in his interaction with the external and internal processing of stimuli" (p. 94).

Summarizing, as an ongoing process while reading, is essential for proficiency. Mature readers use visual and semantic cues to summarize without conscious intent. The indented paragraph, conjunctions, anaphoras, and transitional phrases signal connectivity and facilitate the organization of ideas. Expert readers expect to find intersentential meaning.

Keena needed to purposefully organize the information she read. After explicitly discussing our intention to find ways to make remembering and understanding easier, we began mediation by tapping into what Keena and her classmates already knew about the concept of categorizing objects in their surroundings; we drew conclusions about how grouping things that are alike enables us to better understand and remember them.

The concept of grouping objects was extended to the idea of grouping or "chunking" sentences using the following sequence:

1. Read aloud and decide sentence by sentence what the sentences in the paragraph are talking about.

2. Decide when the sentences are no longer talking about the same thing.

3. Label the connected sentences with their topic (See Chapter 10 for a sample lesson).

In order for Keena to maintain awareness of chunking information while reading independently, she was taught to record her organization of the text in a semantic hierarchy map, shown in Figure 6.3. Figure 6.4 shows a 3rd grader's semantic map for chapter notes.

Graphic organizers provide a valuable bridge between left-brain language processing and right-brain visual, global processing, and this particular graphic organizer creates the perfect footprint for text representation. Reading from top to bottom and left to right, students have a record of the topic and its subtopics in the order they appear in the text. Note taking in this way requires seeking

Figure 6.3 | **Semantic Hierarchy Map for Note Taking**

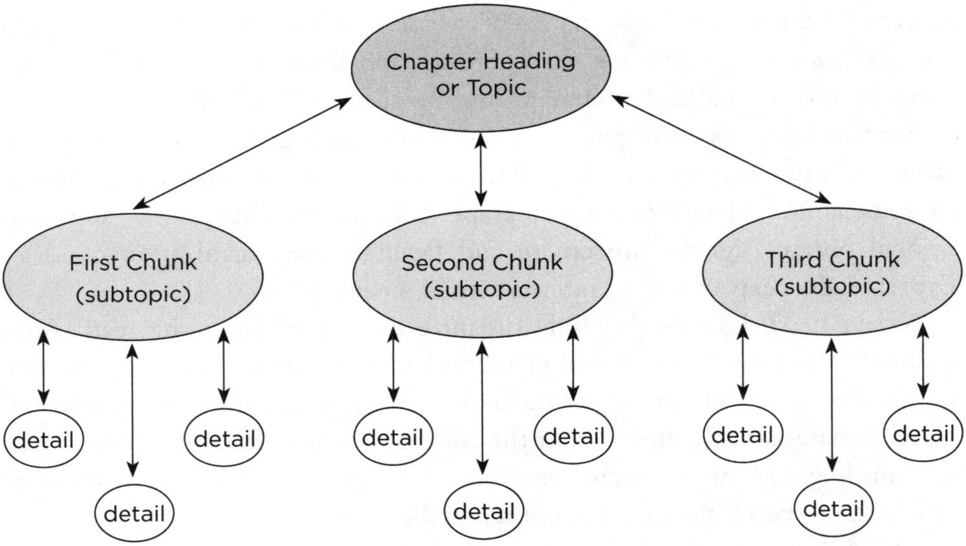

```
                        Chapter Heading
                           or Topic


    First Chunk           Second Chunk           Third Chunk
    (subtopic)            (subtopic)             (subtopic)


 detail     detail     detail     detail     detail     detail

      detail                detail                detail
```

connections and inferring what those connections are. Instead of viewing narrative or expository writing as a string of details, the overdifferentiating reader learns to perceive the structure and design of the text in a meaning-making way.

Once students learn how to respond to their reading, their reading response journals become another appendage. Students reach for their pens and notebooks when they start to read. Some students like filling the page with bubbles bulging with their notes; others prefer a linear format and start to list the "chunks" as they read. The second of Keena's journal entries (see Figure 6.2) reflects the transition in her perception of the text. She listed the flow of events instead of producing a verbatim duplication of the sentences. Keena's ability to generate her own questions indicated that she was finally interacting with what she was reading, and her spontaneous recall during book discussions affirmed for Keena that she had become a better reader.

Semantic maps are useful for constructing written summaries of the material the students read. When working cooperatively to summarize research

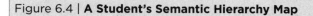

Figure 6.4 | **A Student's Semantic Hierarchy Map**

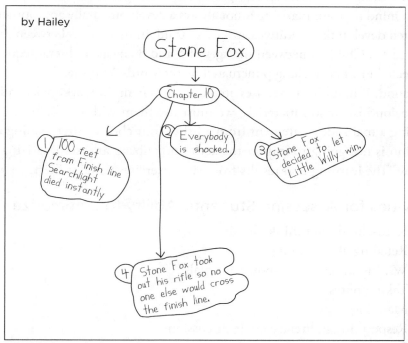

Student work used by permission.

material or prepare a book talk, students applied the criteria we had developed during guided practice:

- Summaries retell the text succinctly by connecting the main ideas' statements.
- Summaries do not require guessing at what is important. They do not require speculation or the subjective selection of parts that are interesting.
- Summaries are the skeleton of a fully elaborated narrative or expository text.

Let's pause to note two points. First, if book reports are going to live on in our classrooms along with other relics like Monday and Friday spelling pretests and retests, we should recognize that requiring students to tell about the plot of a chapter book in one paragraph is a hefty job of summarizing. Explicit instruction in writing summaries should precede such assignments. It is important to bear in mind that summarizing is not always a developmentally appropriate task. Children develop the cognitive capacity to think in main ideas between the ages of 8 and 11. Children between the ages of 5 and 8 engage in literal sequencing, as reflected in story retelling punctuated by the words "and then."

Second, if main-idea exercises are going to remain in workbooks and comprehension instruction materials, we must use them with full knowledge that selecting a main-idea statement from a list of four choices after reading a brief selection is not going to impact the act of organizing and summarizing while reading. The learning that results from such exercises remains inert.

Activities for Assessing Students' Ability to Summarize

- Read-alouds and think-alouds
- Retelling after reading
- Writing in reading response journals
- Taking notes
- Mapping
- Responding in literary circle discussions
- Responding in teacher-student conferences
- Summarizing chapters and books
- Differentiating scenes in order to dramatize narrative material
- Charting plot structure
- Locating information for research and question answering
- Using intersentential meaning to infer the meaning of unfamiliar words

Demonstrations of Students' Ability to Summarize

Students demonstrate their ongoing organization of ideas while reading when they

- Retell what they have read with an emphasis on accurately sequenced main ideas.

- Construct graphic organizers that represent the structure of the text accurately.
- Summarize text succinctly.
- Locate information purposefully and quickly using their awareness of the organization of the text.

Asking Self-Generated Questions

The guides that accompany the basal series of old and literature anthologies of today are paved with blocks of questions to be posed by teachers before, during, and after reading. Although I would be among the first to make the case for just how powerful and formative questions can be in shaping thinking, I also believe that the more we question our students when they read, the less opportunity they have to ask their own questions and seek their own answers. Asking questions may ultimately clarify the message of the text, but teacher-directed effort to help students construct meaning does not carry them beyond the specific piece of material at hand. Asking comprehension questions is not teaching comprehension (Durkin, 1978–79). Ultimately, students must ask their own questions in order to be highly interactive and proficient readers.

Strategy Anatomy

When we turn our focus on the learner as question-asker, we see layers of complexity within this reading behavior. Several factors influence the degree to which a reader thinks of questions while reading. First and foremost, we have to attend to the important issues of engagement and self-management. We monitor our reading for understanding when we are reading with a sense of purpose, a high-level interest, and a feeling of ownership and control (Marzano et al., 1988). I believe that when we ask students, "What questions do you have?" and their shoulders reach for their ears, we have to address these prerequisite issues before we start raising awareness of the kinds of questions proficient readers ask.

The transactional model for mediation, when taught in the context of a constructivist classroom, is perfectly suited for the intricate task of meshing motivation, personal control, and explicit instruction. In that setting, the idiosyncratic nature of the learner is central to instructional planning. When students select texts that interest them, understand that problem solving is part of reading, and guide their own book discussions, interactive, responsive reading ensues.

Engagement and motivation increase exponentially when students and teachers read and think aloud. It turns out that asking questions is contagious. Reading and thinking aloud in the company of others generates excitement and proliferates questions in the way a healthy debate scoops up everyone in the room. Within a very short time, the shoulder-shruggers are contributing to the flood of questions.

When students ask very few questions or ask a very narrow range of questions of themselves and the text, we can provide explicit instruction of question-asking strategies. The model lesson is a demonstration of how to examine the text with detective-like scrutiny, keeping an eye out for ambiguity, foreshadowing, and hints of missing information. The teacher shows how she continually checks in with herself as she reads and formulates questions based on the following observations:

- Curiosity about what will come next
- Discrepancies in the text
- Discrepancies that arise between her point of view or schema and the information in the text
- Unfamiliar ideas or information
- Personal connections or concerns
- Interest in unstated outcomes, consequences, and hypothetical possibilities

We want to model questions that seek out personal connections to the text and reveal the unknown. When using expository material, our questions stem from our search for causes, consequences, comparisons, the desire to construct a tableau of a particular time and place, and ultimately an understanding of how what we are learning is relevant to our own lives. Asking open-ended questions that suggest the need for further investigation provides a valuable model for real-world work.

When a greater level of structure is necessary, the teacher models how she stops at the bottom of each page and decides what she wants to know before turning the page. Group practice, buddy reading, and independent journaling provide a framework for practicing question-generating behaviors while reading. The follow-up questions and discussion validates the importance and the merit of asking thoughtful questions while reading.

Ultimately, we want our students to apply and transfer the cognitive behavior of generating questions to all the information and issues that surround them. Preparing our students to question ideas, information, and actions because of the absence of solid reasoning, credible evidence, and well-founded conclusions should be a critical priority.

Activities for Assessing Students' Use of Self-Generated Questions

Any time we want to know whether students are internalizing our instruction, we need to take a seat on the sidelines. The following activities provide opportunities for us to gauge students' use of self-generated questions while reading:

- Read-alouds and think-alouds
- Double-entry journals
- Literary circle discussion
- Teacher-student conferences
- Cooperative research projects

Demonstrations of Students' Use of Self-Generated Questions

- Asking a variety of questions when they read
- Asking questions that indicate they are monitoring their understanding
- Asking questions that examine the author's intent
- Asking questions that reflect an interest in what is coming next

- Asking questions that reflect an interest in knowing the outcome of events
- Asking questions that probe for more information
- Asking questions that show a search for the resolution of discrepancies between their personal experience and what is in the text
- Asking questions that will carry their investigations beyond the text

Monitoring and Using Fix-Up Strategies to Repair Comprehension

When speaking to my graduate students about teaching children to monitor their reading and use fix-up strategies to maintain meaning, I always began with a reading from Toni Morrison's *Beloved*. That particular book co-exists in my mind as both an extraordinary work of prose and a work that I struggled to understand, although I loved the beauty of the cadence of the words and the power of the emotions they evoked. I wanted my class to tease out the strategies a reader can use when challenged in that way.

That was until my not-so-trusty laptop computer helped me realize I had been omitting an essential part of understanding and implementing this key strategy. One moment I was lurching along, writing, deleting, writing, cutting, pasting, and writing and the next moment it was all gone! Gone! What key did I strike? How could this happen? I was in a panic and clueless about what I could do to retrieve my work. I sat there, regarding the keyboard as if it were an alien enemy, too frightening to touch. After an interminable stretch of time, I took the only option I could come up with: I proceeded to save, close, and file. The last thing I saw before the screen went black was a message in Korean followed by an encrypted text confirming my alien theory.

What happened to the fairly self-reliant individual I regarded myself to be? Why couldn't I come up with a productive response to my computer crisis? Where were my fix-up strategies? People, in general, attribute success to ability, effort, luck, and task difficulty (Marzano, 2003). However, Marzano explains "Of these, effort is the most useful because a strong belief in effort as a cause of success can translate into a willingness to engage in complex tasks and persist over time" (p. 146). My computer fiasco tells me we cannot separate building a knowledge base of fix-up strategies from creating a climate that encourages and promotes extending effort. The following practices invite effort:

1. Create a classroom that does not avoid "mistakes." While striving for accuracy, welcome the information that wrong turns and careless errors provide. Today's problem is tomorrow's process lesson.

2. View the classroom as a community that enjoys and supports the process of problem solving. Each unknown is an opportunity to learn or practice ways of finding out what we need to know.

3. Avoid shutting down students' thinking by
   ° Automatically correcting answers.
   ° Asking "Who knows the right answer?" after the "wrong" one is given.
   ° Saying, "No" or "Not quite."
   ° Asking, "Weren't you listening?"

4. Use prompts (see Chapter 1) that consign responsibility to their students to keep trying:
   ° What is one way you can find the information you need?
   ° Did that sound right?
   ° What can you do to make the problem easier to understand?

5. Teach students that faster is not better. Show them that really successful people reflect and take time to get things right.

6. Teach students that changing their mind in the light of new evidence and information is the mark of intelligence.

7. Commit to the paradigm that supporting students' understanding of effective learning processes empowers them in the long term, and correcting answers and word recognition errors is only useful in the short term.

Strategy Anatomy

Awareness and Knowledge

To activate fix-up strategies, students must maintain awareness of what they are supposed to be accomplishing when they read. We can think of that challenge by envisioning putting a jigsaw puzzle together with or without the picture of the completed puzzle in front of us. It is exceedingly difficult to put a complex puzzle together without the image of the whole to guide us. You can place the holistic image of the proficient reader in front of your students with explicit instruction.

Monitoring and Self-Regulation Learning

Monitoring comprehension requires putting awareness into action. It is the difference between knowing and doing. The practices of checking in with yourself to assess if your objectives are being met, deciding if a change in approach has to be made, selecting an adjustment that would be appropriate, and evaluating the outcome of your efforts have to be the subject of explicit mediation as well. So while your strategy instruction is adding to your students' repertoire of essential behaviors, your modeling and discussion of self-regulation demonstrate how to select and apply those strategies when comprehension breaks down. Students know when to

• Stop reading because a word does not make sense and do some word solving (e.g., using phonemic cues, word analysis, linking strategies, and research strategies).

• Keep reading or rerun what they have read in order to figure out what word would make sense (i.e., use semantic cues).

• Reread because a sentence or a passage was confusing.

• Reread because the syntax of a sentence sounds awkward.

• Review a paragraph if they did not get the message and put its message together.

• Look for the connections between paragraphs to get the thrust or flow of the text if those connections are not apparent to them.

• Pay attention to the gaps in information, and formulate questions or attempt to fill them in with their own thinking.

• Review their reading if a message is not evident to them.

• Expend more effort to make sense of the text by adjusting reading pace, taking notes, or using available resources.

Gradual Release of Control

The gradual release of control, discussed in Chapter 3, is essential for self-regulation. SRL strategies can be reinforced by peers in cooperative groups and reading buddy arrangements when the objectives for learning include the use of fix-up strategies as well as the task itself.

When students start working independently, they should have varied venues for responding to their reading that afford them opportunities to check in with themselves and assess their own understanding and performance. Activities that serve that purpose include:

- Drawing what has been envisioned
- Constructing a graphic organizer that reflects the structure and content of the text
- Paraphrasing text
- Journaling reactions and questions

Activities for Assessing Students' Monitoring and Use of Fix-Up Strategies

- Running records that reveal self-corrections and word-solving strategies
- Read-alouds and think-alouds
- Students' rubrics
- Teacher-student conferences
- Cooperative group work

Demonstrations of Students' Monitoring and Use of Fix-Up Strategies

- Asking fewer questions and requesting less help when completing a task
- Showing improved literal and inferential comprehension
- Increasing the use of self-dialogue:
  - "I'm going back to see what I missed. I know I missed something."
  - "There were so many characters I had to make stick-figure drawings and label them so I didn't get mixed up."

- ○ "I figured out what *consequences* means."
- ○ "At first I didn't know who was talking, so I read it over looking for the quotation marks."
- Initiating questions and reactions before, during, and after reading
- Stopping to reflect, question, and summarize while reading

Synthesizing Text and Determining Important Themes

Fountas and Pinnell (2001) define synthesizing as the bringing together of information from the text and from personal, world, and literary knowledge to create new understanding. My granddaughter Jillian taught me something about synthesizing when she was just 6 years old. It was bedtime at Grandma's house, so Jillian selected the books that would be read, except now that she was nearing the end of 1st grade, she would be the reader and Grandma would be read to. She proceeded to read aloud in her teacher voice and turn the book around for her class of one to see. When she had finished the books, I had a light bulb moment: "I just realized," I said with genuine surprise, "these very different stories have the same message." Jillian didn't hesitate in responding. "You should always be yourself," she said with an air of finality.

Jillian's fluid word recognition, her familiarity with the landscape of literature—characters, plots, settings, story problems—and her expectation that stories teach a lesson made her conclusion about the two unrelated stories a natural consequence of her reading.

Strategy Anatomy

I tell my students that reading without thinking about the theme of the text is like chewing your food but not swallowing it. Chewing allows us to enjoy the rich flavors and textures of the food, but without swallowing and digesting the food, we would not absorb what we have consumed—the food would not nourish and enrich us.

Inferring the theme of narrative or expository material is the apex of the reading process. To synthesize everything from the surface structure of the text to the wilderness of inferences, reactions, questions, conclusions, explanations, predictions, and judgments that we conjure along the way, we use a laundry list of thinking behaviors. The more complex the text, the more acrobatic the act of synthesizing becomes. As we construct the theme of complex material, the following mental operations may come into play:

- Gathering data
- Classifying
- Correlational reasoning
- Monitoring
- Explaining
- Inferring—predicting, analyzing, judging, hypothesizing, generalizing
- Comparing

Jillian's effortless response to my observation that the two books she read have the same message is a demonstration that children do synthesize information without our intervention and instruction. I believe that ability is a consequence of our minds being wired to organize and make meaning of the information we take in. However, we can't sit this one out. We have two indispensable roles to play if our students are going to take their understanding of text to the highest level. First, as good coaches, we must support conversations about literature that encourage the integration and production of ideas. Second, as mediators, we have to be ready to provide explicit instruction when the text our students are reading resists their efforts to synthesize its message.

Supporting Conversations That Synthesize Text

If we are going to ask our students questions about their reading, we have to take responsibility for framing their thinking about books. I ascribe to the Great Books approach, which launches book conversations with an interpretive question (i.e., questions that do not have one definitive answer). Questions like these ask students to react to the book as a whole:

- Why do you think Jack succeeded in his quest even though he made so many bad choices?

• Why do you think Boris and Amos were such good friends even though they are so different?
• Why do you think the author used the title she did for this story?

The Great Books questions are not just global questions; they are questions that require the reader to consider the ambiguities and complexities of the story. Information can be found to support differing answers. Once the students have summarized the story, and any confusion or misunderstanding has been clarified, all readers, regardless of their word recognition ability, can participate in the discussion. The exploration of the synthesizing questions invariably leads back into the text at its most basic, literal level.

Explicit Mediation

What do we do when we synthesize the theme of a piece of literature? Because so many variables contribute to the creation of the overall message of a story or book, it is likely that each of us would answer that question somewhat differently. When analyzing a complex strategy, it is best to simplify the problem. In my classes, I start with an Aesop fable. The following sequence for explicit instruction is appropriate for upper primary and intermediate students.

1. Clarify the concept of theme with a study of fables. The moral of the story is explicitly stated.
2. Determine the story message with a study of fairytales. The flat characters and the predictable story endings illustrate how the character's traits and the character's fate convey the message (e.g., kindness is rewarded).
3. Infer the story message by working backward. Using folktales with a clear message, identify what story elements were used to convey the theme.

When working with intermediate and secondary students, the think-aloud should emphasize the problem-solving nature of determining the theme of a story and the point that each reader may view the book's message differently. When helping students infer the author's message, stress the possibility that there is more than one important theme. Thinking of the author as a puppeteer who controls everything that happens in the book, review the ways the author talks to us:

- The narration
- The characters' words, thoughts, actions, traits, beliefs, experiences, and points of view
- The events woven into the plot and how those events affect the characters
- The story problems and their resolutions

Constructing a graphic organizer to arrange the information gathered from each of the story elements clarifies this multifaceted strategy and facilitates drawing conclusions. Using the analogy of a spider web is useful to intermediate students for synthesizing the plot structure of a book. After drawing a web with its supporting bridge across the center and the many spokes emanating from it, the students work collaboratively to determine the book's central story line and its subplots. That perspective of the book's structure facilitates the conversation about the author's intent.

Activities for Assessing Students' Ability to Synthesize Text and Infer Important Themes

- Literature response discussions
- Written responses to reading
- Double-entry journals
- Read-alouds and think-alouds
- Student-led discussions
- Selecting source material for research

Demonstrations of Students' Ability to Synthesize Text and Infer Important Themes

I want to know if my students are

- Comparing story themes.
- Selecting texts that are relevant to a chosen topic.

- Discussing the author's point of view.
- Determining the information that is important to the theme.
- Explaining how characters' words and actions convey the author's message.
- Identifying the literary devices that convey the author's message.
- Determining if the author is speaking through the narrator.
- Comparing the author's message with their own beliefs and attitudes.
- Asking questions as a result of acquiring a new perspective from their reading.

A Consideration

Each time we share our understanding of what is "under the hood" with our students we take one step closer to the day they will no longer wait for test results and report cards to find out how they are doing and what they have learned. Imagine.

7

LOOKING UNDER THE HOOD:
KEY WRITING STRATEGIES

It was an epiphany for me. When I finished reading *Lessons from a Child,* Lucy Calkins's (1983) chronicle of her research in two New Hampshire elementary school classrooms, I really got it. I had a grasp of how to make writing about the writer. With each page, the era of composition on demand and red-lined corrections slipped further and further away. Calkins introduced me to a fresh vision of students striving to improve their writing because it was *their* writing— stories and topics they had chosen. I had accompanied her to classrooms in which teachers learned how to teach best by being open to learning from their students. They conferred with their student writers, giving them feedback to consider and options to choose. I witnessed 1st and 3rd graders expand their awareness of the writer's craft and gain control of their written words with earnest enthusiasm.

Understanding that writers need to be in a community, Calkins and her colleagues created writing workshops in which children wrote, listened to each other, and learned from the models presented by their teachers in 5- to 10-minute lessons. These minilessons brought explicit instruction to the teaching of writing. They placed the teacher in front of her students in order to demonstrate, explain, and clarify effective writing behaviors. All of these innovations inform our work with explicit transactional mediation. The following points summarize the understandings, commitments, and practices that we bring to our mediation of writing behaviors from Calkins's teachings:

1. Writing is approached as a problem-solving process. Students learn how to strive for flexibility, persistence, and accuracy. Teachers model problem solving such as showing how to replace repeated words; how to get beyond short, choppy sentences; how to clarify mixed-up writing; how to avoid too much or too little information; and how to rearrange confusing sentences.

2. Students learn the steps of the writing process so that they can guide themselves through topic selection, planning organization, drafting, revising, and proofreading. While teachers structure the writing environment, the workshop, and the direct instruction, they gradually release control of the writing process to students.

3. Students have a clear understanding of what constitutes good writing. They are provided with exemplars, and they can identify the criteria those samples meet.

4. When students are developmentally ready, they maintain two perspectives or two frames of reference when they write: they can alternate between being a writer and being a reader of writing.

5. Students understand and appreciate that expanding their repertoire of revision strategies changes and improves their writing. They know that revision is an ongoing process of reshaping writing; it is not a consequence of making mistakes or writing poorly. They see that the learning is in the doing, not simply in the getting done.

6. Teachers coach their students. They ask open questions that encourage students to make their own decisions, such as these:
   ○ Where can your new information go?
   ○ How will you convey how you were feeling?
   ○ What are some ways you can grab your readers' attention?

7. Students learn how to give and receive constructive feedback. They learn that feedback has to be specific and respectful.

What knowledge and understanding must we bring to the writing workshop so that we can guide our students into becoming proficient writers? What are the criteria for effective communication? What standards inform our assessments and interventions? This chapter takes a closer look at six nonnegotiable criteria for successful writing. Using age-appropriate explicit instruction, we need to be able to teach our students strategies necessary for

- Maintaining focus and theme.
- Organizing ideas and maintaining coherence.
- Elaborating with specific and relevant supporting details.
- Using effective words, sentence structure, and sentence variety.
- Utilizing vivid and specific vocabulary.
- Controlling the conventions of print.

Darren, a 4th grade student, is going to help us examine these writing strategies and some of our options for providing explicit transactional mediation when it is needed. We will see what we can learn from Darren's first draft and the revisions he makes after receiving feedback from his fellow writers and explicit instruction on elaboration that slows down the action for dramatic effect. Which criteria of effective communication does Darren's writing demonstrate? What strategies did he use in his revisions to meet those criteria?

Darren's Draft

It was the night of the 18th. August 18th that is. We were going to the Yankee game. My Dad and two brothers were coming with me. I got ready at 5:00, left at 5:35. The game started at 7:30. We got there at 7:00. It took us fifteen minutes to find a parking space. We bought a hat, went in, found our seats, sat down and tried to enjoy the fresh air of the Bronx.

My brothers and I decided we wanted a hot dog and a coke, one for each. Skipping the 1st, 2nd, 3rd, and 4th inings we come to the 5th ining. A very important ining. I had finished my hot dog and half the coke. Now the story might have been boring but here comes an exciting part. Alex Rodriguez the Great was up. (A-Rod for short.) Well anyway

A-Rod was up. Ball one called the umpire. Ball two called the umpire. Strike one then. Now the moment we've all been waiting for, A-Rod, his 2nd Grand Slam of the season. There the ball was, coming right at me at 20 mph. I caught it. No, I missed it by an inch. My Coke spilled. I cried. I missed the ball. Oh woe is me, woe is me. Right after I missed the ball, I went to the bathroom and put a band-aid on each of my fingers. I've never got a chance like that to get a baseball. But for now on, every baseball game I go to, I bring a glove.

Darren's Revision

My First Baseball—Almost

It was the night of August 16th. My dad, two brothers, and I were going to the Yankee Game at Yankee Stadium. The game started at 7:30, so we had to hurry because it was 6:45.

When we got there, we bought a hat, went in, found our seats, sat down, and tried to enjoy the not-so-fresh air of the Bronx. My brothers and I decided that we wanted a hot dog and a Coke—one for each. Skipping the first, second, third, and fourth inings, we come to the fifth ining (a very important ining.) I had finished my hot dog and half the Coke.

Alex Rodriguez the Great was up (A-Rod for short). Well anyway, A-Rod was up. "Ball one!" called the umpire. "Ball two!" (I would think the umpire was getting tired of calling balls, so finally he yelled, "Strike!") A-Rod was getting mad now. I think A-Rod took it out on the ball, he hit a home run! At the crack of the bat, I knew something was going to happen. As A-Rod was circling the bases, I saw a small, white blur with red stripes coming at me at the speed of a comet. It was coming at me in a sort of circle-ly path, so I had to keep my eye on it or else, maybe, BONK! My brothers were screaming because of the noise, but it was like I was in another world—just me and the ball. It was getting very close now, so I decided to stand and put my hand up to try to catch it. The ball was about to hit my hand and when it did, I almost screamed!

It hurt so much, I thought I was dying. I caught it! At that second I thought how many people would see this on T.V. This was going to be a great moment in my life. I had to catch this ball. I just had to! Oh no! It went right through my hand! My Coke spilled, I cried, I missed the ball! I'm not famous—I'm a failure! Oh, woe is me!

Right after I missed the ball, I went to the bathroom and put a band-aid on each of my fingers because my hand hurt. The band-aids made a kind of glove. I've never gotten a chance like that again to get an Alex Rodriguez-hit baseball, but from then on, every baseball game I go to, I BRING A GLOVE!

Maintaining Focus and Theme

Strategy Anatomy

Nothing derails communication more than when the assembled words do not have direction or maintain a focus. Reading such writing can be as disconcerting as encountering an abstract painting for the first time and expecting the surface of the canvas to tell a story, but the painting's colors and shapes lack the cohesiveness you anticipate. You're left shaking your head and saying, "I just don't get it."

We do get Darren's piece. It consistently moves his readers to the event he intended to relate—the missed A-Rod baseball. He does not fall into the familiar traps. Some writers veer from their topic never to return, giving their readers something analogous to a stream of consciousness. Others, particularly when answering a question or expressing a point of view, miss their target altogether and address a somewhat related topic. Very often, young writers have difficulty establishing the boundaries of their topic. They include details or events that are tangentially related but irrelevant to the focus of the writing. I characterize such writing as A to Z stories.

Darren's first two paragraphs provide a setting for his story and start to build momentum for the climactic scene. We never felt like we were wandering around the Bronx without a destination. Equally important, I believe, is the reader's ability to see or infer why Darren wanted to tell this story. His voice conveys the excitement and disappointment of what he believes to be a once-in-a-lifetime near brush with fame. Before getting into the mechanics of maintaining focus, student writers should be asked to consider why they have selected their topics and if the thought of writing on the topic makes them feel excited. From a pragmatic perspective, finding the energy in their stories helps students make revision decisions.

When we look under the hood to clarify this vital aspect of good writing, we see that keeping writing focused requires identifying the main point of the piece and then selecting related supporting ideas and information. It is a task of classifying information and differentiating between superordinate and subordinate ideas. Explicit instruction, therefore, needs to go beyond talking about staying on the topic. Students who have difficulty in this area need to learn a strategy for keeping their eye on the ball. The semantic hierarchy map that we used to organize and summarize text is an ideal tool because (1) students can apply what they have learned about the organization of text to their own writing and (2) that particular graphic organizer creates a footprint for the construction of paragraphs.

Constructing a semantic map before writing creates an opportunity to make careful, considered choices regarding what information, events, or ideas support the topic in the bubble at the top of the page. The map then serves as a guide to be referred to when drafting each paragraph. When revising, the map anchors decisions about whether material is aligned with the focus of the piece or not.

Activities for Assessing Students' Ability to Maintain Focus

- Extended responses to literature
- Personal narratives
- Informational writing
- Instructions and procedures
- Descriptive writing
- Book reviews
- Letters expressing requests or complaints
- Biographical and autobiographical writing
- Oral reports

Demonstrations of Students' Ability to Maintain Focus

- Narratives and expository writing support one topic.
- Answers pertain to the question asked.
- Research is selective and has a thesis.
- The writing of directions and instructions avoids descriptive or subjective information.
- Prompted responses to literature stay within the parameters of the text.
- Letter writing or online correspondence conveys the intended message.
- Oral presentations are cogent.

Organizing Ideas and Maintaining Coherence

Does Darren's piece demonstrate a need to learn strategies for organizing writing? Does his story leave you lost or confused in any way? Does he use appropriate signal words to connect ideas and cue the reader? The external organization of the story conveys the sequence of his narrative. The four paragraphs in his revised piece reflect his awareness of a story structure that includes an introduction, a beginning, a middle, and an end. He tries to maintain continuity and presents events in a logical order from the time he arrives at the ballpark until the conclusion of the missed-ball incident. He creates a transition with the sentence "Skipping the first, second, third, and fourth innings. . . ."

Within the climax of his story, however, I experience some confusion. He thinks he caught the ball. Then he's hoping he catches the ball. Then he realized the ball went through his hand. His succession of short sentences, the use of exclamation marks, and the strong language (e.g., *dying, screaming, great moment, cried*) create the mood of hurried excitement we would expect at a moment like the one Darren is describing. Is Darren aware of this glitch in the internal organization of that paragraph? If the way he wrote it is the way he remembers it, could Darren figure out a way to let us know things did get confusing, and his writing is a reflection of that?

Strategy Anatomy

Well-organized writing often seems like the last frontier that otherwise good writers need to conquer. From elementary age students to doctoral candidates, organization is surprisingly and frequently weak.

Advance planning is an antidote to poorly organized writing, but only if the writer has learned how to organize in advance. Some practices that are commonly used to help students organize their ideas are actually ineffective and nonproductive. One of those is the array or web. This spider-like graphic organizer is used in conjunction with the brainstorming phase of the writing process. However, while the splash of ideas on the page puts the story content on display, the overall organization and the internal organization of the writing is left to work itself out somehow.

Another staple for helping students learn organizing skills is teaching them to recognize the five patterns of organization. Students typically receive printed material that differentiates writing that (1) lists or describes, (2) compares and contrasts, (3) shows cause and effect, (4) sequences events, and (5) discusses problems and solutions. Each pattern is accompanied by a compatible graphic organizer and the appropriate signal words. Students use the graphic and the signal words to prepare their five representative pieces of writing.

What is missing from these instructional approaches? Are these lessons clarifying the concept of organization, or are they providing examples of patterns to be copied? Are students being made aware of the decisions a writer makes when organizing his or her ideas? Do these lessons give students declarative knowledge without the procedural knowledge they need to put that information to work when they are writing independently?

Explicit mediation has to begin with clarifying the underlying concept of categorizing information. Ideally, students have already been taught how to summarize text and have learned that written information is organized. They have sorted and grouped concrete objects, such as a pile of assorted blocks or writing implements, in order to understand the process of categorizing, and they recognize the clarity that results from grouping like things.

For students who are challenged to express their ideas cogently, the explicit, highly structured mediation process listed here is a valuable investment to make:

1. Identify the topic of the writing.
2. "Dump" all the information you have in a list.
3. Start grouping the details you have generated by selecting one detail and looking for another detail that is connected to the first one in some way.

Circle matching details with the same color marker. The following is an example of thinking aloud while organizing the details for a character sketch of Mrs. Green from Mike Thaler's *The Teacher from the Black Lagoon*:

> "Mrs. Green has a tail. What would go with that detail? Hmmm, scratchy claws? I think they go together because they both tell about her unusual looks. They describe her."

4. Continue looking for details that belong in the same category and circling them with the same color.

5. Before going on to plan the draft, ask students to think-pair-share about why the details have been circled in different colors.

6. Model and think aloud as you organize the subtopics and details on a semantic map.

7. Decide on how you will order your writing.

> "What would my reader need to know first about Mrs. Green? Would it be more helpful to know one of the things she did in class, or should I start with telling who she is? Maybe people should know she is a mean and scary creature who will be the teacher for the day. That way my audience will understand the things that happen in the story."

8. Number the sequence of the sentences or paragraphs you have decided on. Experiment with different possibilities.

9. Decide on the sequence of details within each subtopic. Consider how inserting conjunctions and combining details affect the smoothness of the writing.

10. Rehearse translating the abbreviated notes in the map into complete well-developed sentences.

For writing that will be three or more paragraphs, rehearsing includes using the map in order to plan the story design. Examples of design decisions include determining whether the story will proceed from beginning to end or whether it will start at the end and flashback to the beginning, how to bridge the paragraphs, whether there are too few or too many details for each paragraph, and where new information should be inserted.

Activities for Assessing Students' Ability to Organize Ideas

- Personal narrative
- Research presentations
- Retelling in reading journals
- Semantic hierarchy maps
- Letter writing

Demonstrations of Students' Ability to Organize Ideas

- Paragraph breaks are used appropriately.
- Related ideas are grouped together.
- Paragraphs have a stated or inferred topic and contain supporting details.
- Material is sequenced in a logical way.
- Coherence is maintained with the use of appropriate transitions.

Elaborating with Specific and Relevant Supporting Details

The thrust of Darren's revisions was the removal of unnecessary details and the incorporation of details surrounding the climactic moment of his story. He returned to his draft after listening to an abridged version of Richard Connell's short story *The Most Dangerous Game*. By applying the author's technique of relating a crucial event in slow motion, one small frame at a time, Darren brought dramatic tension to his writing. Good models taken from good literature demonstrate the power of richly elaborated actions, descriptions, emotions, and ideas.

Strategy Anatomy

Elaboration is one of those big words, like *metamorphosis,* that kids love to say, but saying it does not make it part of their writing repertoire. We could just prompt students to write well-developed ideas instead of writing in a list fashion by saying, "Tell more" or "Do you think you could help us to see what you are describing?" However, if students are going to monitor their own writing and revision, what do they need to know? What will signal them that they indeed do have to tell more?

To begin with, students must understand the concept of specific and general. To build that understanding we can start by helping students identify the generic words in their writing so they can replace them with more specific and vivid language. Explicit instruction that includes mapping familiar words clarifies the distinction between general and specific words. Two examples of such maps are shown in Figure 7.1.

Once students have demonstrated that they can recognize the general terms in their writing, they can begin to follow the teacher's model for replacing those words with more specific and descriptive language. For example:

I saw a <u>boat</u> in the <u>water.</u>
I saw a <u>canoe</u> in the <u>river.</u>
I saw a <u>battered canoe</u> in the <u>raging river.</u>

To go beyond using minimal language, students also need to become accustomed to engaging in divergent thinking so that they can generate details that inform, clarify, illuminate, and enhance the message. A round-robin activity, like the one that follows, is one way to mediate divergent and elaborative thinking.

Teacher: I had so much homework last night! Can you elaborate?
Student 1: There were 20 pages of math examples.
Student 2: They were all long division in the thousands.
Student 3: Then I had to read 50 pages in my social studies book.

A teacher-directed group writing experience that incorporates the students' elaborative thinking provides scaffolded instruction and prepares students for applying what they have learned to their own writing. For example:

Original sentence: John ate a candy bar.
Elaborated sentence: John devoured the Snickers in one bite. His cheeks bulged like a chipmunk getting ready for winter. A look of sweet satisfaction washed over his face as he licked the last of the chocolate from his sticky lips.

Once students understand the concept of elaboration, explicit transactional instruction is used to experiment and problem solve with making choices that

Figure 7.1 | **General and Specific Words**

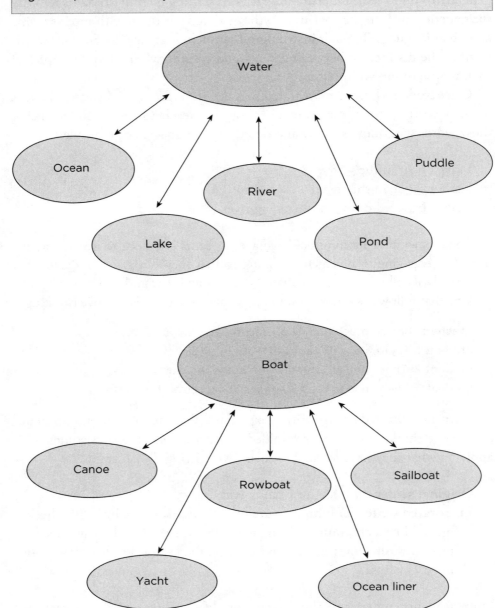

are necessary for well-developed writing. Elaboration that clarifies and enhances stated ideas and information is partly a function of the writer's ability to recognize the absence of supporting details. This is easier to address during the planning or mapping stage of writing when skimpy paragraphs can be readily spotted. You know your explicit teaching has been internalized when you hear students talk about elaboration in their conferences and when you see students exercise the mental self-management required for independent revisions of poorly developed writing.

Activities for Assessing Students' Use of Elaboration

- Letters to friends, organizations, and businesses
- Narrative writing
- Research and reporting
- Extended responses to literature

Demonstrations of Students' Use of Elaboration

- The writer does not list information.
- Declarative statements are followed with description, explanation, and analysis.
- The reader can visualize people, places, and things in the writing.
- The reader can understand the author's feelings, attitudes, and views.
- Language is specific.
- Persuasive writing goes beyond stating a point of view and provides ample supporting statements.

Using Effective Words, Sentence Structure, and Sentence Variety

The paradigm shift on which the use of explicit transactional mediation depends meets its greatest resistance in the next two areas we are about to explore. Language use and the conventions of print have been taught predominantly through memorization and drill. New words and their definitions; rules of grammar, usage, punctuation, capitalization, and spelling have been the domain of transmission education. If I were to channel Dr. Phil of TV fame, I would ask those attached to the old order, "How's that workin' for ya?"

The Effective Use of Words: Strategy Anatomy

On the subject of vocabulary, Fountas and Pinnell (2001) write:

> The development of vocabulary is such an enormous achievement that experts are not sure of the precise process involved. The average elementary school student probably learns about three thousand words a year (Nagy, 1988). We do know that a great number of new words come from the reading that takes place yet traditionally vocabulary is taught by asking students to look words up in the dictionary and write their definitions. (p. 376)

Anyone who has spent an extended period of time in a classroom has come across gems of insufficiently learned new vocabulary such as the following:

The fireman <u>frugaled</u> the baby from the burning building.
The class <u>migrated</u> to recess.
When I saw my grandparents, I gave them a big <u>smirk</u> and ran to them.

Increasing vocabulary and applying those words to one's writing sounds more simple than it is. As Fountas and Pinnell (2001) explain, there are many ways to "know" a word. Knowing a word requires placing it within a rich network of understanding that includes multiple meanings, subtle shades of meaning, connotations, figurative expressions, even historical origins or geographically specific meanings. "Words and the concepts they convey don't stand alone; they are bound by meaningful relationships with other words" (pp. 375–376). If you really know a word, you can

- Read it in many different contexts, understanding the meaning each time.
- Use the word appropriately when speaking or writing.
- Realize the connotations (implied meanings) that a word may have when used in a certain way (e.g., as part of irony or sarcasm).
- Use the word metaphorically if appropriate.

Research findings by Beck and McKeown (1991) and Stahl and Fairbanks (1986) support the conclusion that students benefit from direct vocabulary instruction but that it must provide repeated exposure to words and provide varied opportunities to experience words in their many facets and contexts (Fountas & Pinnell, 2001).

Word study activities are valuable for the opportunities they give students to learn words using a wide variety of print and resource materials. Investigating words cooperatively, students gather information about a word's origins, multiple meanings, connotations, shades of meaning, and figurative use. They devise maps to organize their findings and explore the connections and associations a word has with their prior knowledge.

The teacher's explicit transactional mediation supports (1) the decision-making process of replacing familiar vocabulary with the new and improved words the students have been studying and (2) judging the appropriateness of new vocabulary relevant to the message being conveyed. Here are some coaching prompts that raise awareness of the criteria for revision:

- "Are there general words you could replace with specific words you have learned that would be more meaningful to a reader who is trying to visualize or understand your message?"
- "Have you repeated words that you could replace with pronouns, proper nouns, or synonyms you have learned?"
- "Have you used hackneyed words that you could 'bury' and replace with vivid words you have learned?"
- "Can you locate places in your writing where exaggeration, similes, metaphors, humor, or stronger language would help get your message across?"

Does Darren's piece suggest that he could benefit from explicit mediation of this kind? His word choices would not earn a high score in a Scrabble game, but he does use some specific and vivid imagery (e.g., "crack of the bat"; "white blur"; "coming at me with the speed of a comet"). I do think Darren's writing could be taken further. The presence of his tongue-in-cheek voice indicates to me that he is in command of his writing. He is ready to challenge himself with the help of some wonderful literature that would model more sophisticated vocabulary.

Activities for Assessing Students' Effective Use of Words

- Personal narratives
- Scripts for dramatization of literature
- Responses to literature
- Extended responses to content area reading
- Letter writing
- Journal entries

Demonstrations of Students' Effective Use of Words

- Avoids repetitive word choice
- Avoids hackneyed vocabulary (e.g., *then, important, good, say, went*)
- Eliminates general, vague language
- Experiments with similes, metaphors, and figurative language
- Uses words that express emotion, tension, excitement, and vivid description

The Effective Use of Sentence Structure and Sentence Variety: Strategy Anatomy

Students may leave our classrooms when they move on to higher grades, but they do not leave their incomplete sentences behind. Those fragments of grammatically complete thoughts may in fact accompany them to the ivory towers that await them. Truth be told, when I was an undergraduate, I had a particular fondness for the dash—not so much for periods.

The students who never get the "complete sentence thing" when they are writing can usually tell you what a sentence is and what its distinguishing punctuation is, and they intuitively understand sentence boundaries. However, transferring this knowledge from the spoken word to the written words resists explanations, practice exercises, and an infinite number of corrections.

The ultimate answer to this quandary may be found in the green wavy line that appears under the text on our computer screens to signal some rule of grammar has been violated and revision is required. The idealists among us may pursue resolution of the incomplete sentence issue by enlisting the wisdom and methodology of explicit transactional mediation.

A student's writing provides a laboratory for teaching how to improve sentence structure and sentence variety. Using explicit mediation, the teacher models and thinks aloud as she searches a piece of writing to

- Differentiate a complete thought (noun phrase and verb phrase) from an incomplete thought by reading a sentence out of context.
- Check for punctuation marks that distinguish the sentences.
- Identify sentences that are long and confusing or short and choppy.
- Decide if the sentences lack variety because they are all short or all long.
- Find sentences that begin with the same word or words.

Locating and identifying the sentence characteristics listed here is dependent on the student's ability to be accurate, thorough, and persistent. Therefore, the explicit teaching and application of these problem-solving behaviors are an integral part of the revision process (see Chapter 8). As students learn to identify sentences that need revision, they need the tools for improvement. Essentially, sentence revision is a dance of moving, combining, and embedding. Here are some examples:

- Moving the order of words, phrases, and clauses to avoid repeating sentence beginnings
- Combining short sentences with the same subject by embedding adjectives
- Embedding defining information using appositive phrases
- Combining short, choppy sentences to create variety and clarify the connection of ideas with conjunctions (e.g., *and, but, however, yet, nor, so, yet*) and subordinating conjunctions (e.g., *because, while, until, before, after, when, though, unless*)

Combining sentences, though a very effective way to elevate the continuity and maturity of expression, may be surprisingly problematic for students who have not benefited from exposure to rich oral and written language in their early years. They may have difficulty assigning meaning to nonconcrete words that function as the "glue" of language. Such lack of exposure is also often a factor in poor reading comprehension. Oral activities to assess which conjunctions should be taught are invaluable prerequisites to explicit instruction of sentence-combining revision strategies. An example follows:

> **Teacher:** Finish my sentence:
> I was going to go swimming today, but _____.
> My bike had a flat tire, so _____.
> My family bought a new house because _____.
> Everyone left the building when _____.
> I usually love to play ball; however, _____.
> My little brother is lots of fun, yet _____.

Activities that provide frequent and varied opportunities to "play" with conjunctions in order to combine sentences can be embedded in writing and reading workshops, morning board work, group editing, and learning centers. The extensive use of these kinds of activities may be necessary before more meaningful and appropriate conjunctions start to replace the word *and* in students' writing.

Would Darren benefit from sentence improvement mediation? The flow of language can obfuscate the failings of an individual sentence. Darren would probably not pick up the following run-on sentence: "The ball was about to hit my hand, when it did, I almost screamed, it hurt so much I thought I was dying." If Darren's teacher chose to mediate Darren's recognition of run-ons, she could start by reading each phrase aloud and punctuating the sentences with pauses.

Activities for Assessing Students' Use of Effective Sentence Structure and Sentence Variety

- Narrative writing
- Content-area writing
- Letter writing
- Extended responses to literature

Demonstrations of Students' Use of Effective Sentence Structure and Sentence Variety

- A sequence of sentences that start differently
- Sentences that stand on their own because they convey a coherent message
- Sentences that are clear
- Sentences of varying length

Controlling the Conventions of Print

The rule-driven nature of usage, grammar, spelling, punctuation, and capitalization and the sheer number of those rules prevent me from giving careful consideration to all the conventions of print in this space. Therefore, I will not be talking about the content of instruction in this area as much as the transactional nature of explicit mediation and the rationale behind it.

Let's begin by taking a closer look at some of the sentences that Darren wrote in the first draft of his story:

- "It was the night of the 16th. August 16th that is."
- "I got ready at 5:00. left at 5:30."
- "Skipping the 1st, 2nd, 3rd, and 4th inings we come to the 5th ining."
- "The ball was about to hit my hand, when it did, I almost screamed, it hurt so much that I thought I was dying."

What do these sentences demonstrate about Darren's knowledge regarding spelling, punctuation, and capitalization? Would you address each of his so-called errors? Which of the following options would you select?

1. Make corrections on his draft so that the final draft will be ready for publication.

2. Teach Darren the rules that apply to his use of capitalization, punctuating with commas, and spelling. Have him memorize the rules, and reinforce his learning with practice exercises.

3. Use good writing models to teach Darren correct form. Ask him to apply what he has learned to his own writing.

4. Guide Darren to inductively arrive at the generalizations he needs to know (e.g., "When a word has a short vowel sound in the last or only syllable, double the final consonant before adding an inflectional ending").

5. Select one or two errors that are reflective of pervasive patterns in his writing. Provide mediation for those types of errors. If the piece is going to be published for a wider audience, address the remaining corrections in the final edit.

Constance Weaver (1996) gives us perspective regarding these choices through her extensive research and study. She has examined the practice of teaching sentence structure and mechanics in isolation in order to improve writing. She cites decades of research that does not support that practice. Those studies conclude that the formal isolated teaching of grammar does not improve students' writing, editing ability, or standardized test results. The alternative is promoting the acquisition of the conventions of writing while engaged in the writing process and minimizing the teaching of rules and the use of terminology. Weaver maintains that effective teaching of grammar in context is accomplished with explicit teaching through discussions, investigations of text, and discovery.

Many conscientious teachers are not comfortable relinquishing their English grammar programs that provide sequenced lessons and practice exercises. Covering the material in the book is equated with thoroughness. They feel their students are being shortchanged without that strand of instruction. Allowing mediation to grow out of demonstrated need seems kind of hit-or-miss. In actuality, as long as writing is an integral part of all facets of the curriculum, it is hard to avoid bumping into our students' needs since what they write shows us what they need to know. If we do not address a need when it arises in a particular piece of writing, we can rest assured that same need will present itself again.

Teaching the mechanics of writing outside the textbook or workbook does not signal that we are being lax or casual about instruction in that area. The connection between clarity and the appropriate use of conventions must be an explicit message and a shared value in the writing workshop. However, students also learn that the conventions of print are the handmaiden to the message.

Although we can teach the conventions of print very effectively without programmed materials, we do need to anchor our transactional instruction with good resources for our lessons. Teachers must have authoritative handbooks on grammar, usage, and mechanics to refer to. Students need a rich assortment of expository material and literature to serve as models for investigation as well as dictionaries, thesauruses, and individual editing checklists.

Explicit Transactional Mediation of the Conventions of Print

Using our model for explicit mediation, Darren and the other students in his 4th grade class who demonstrate a need to recognize and eliminate sentence fragments in their writing would receive instruction containing the following components:

- Following the focusing conversation in the model lesson, the teacher writes and thinks aloud about her decisions to punctuate with commas or periods. She notes (1) pronouns are subjects, too; (2) phrases that begin with *when, until, because, unless,* and *before* are not complete sentences; and (3) complete sentences must have a subject, a verb or verb phrase, and a predicate.
- Students retell the process that they observed.
- For group practice, the teacher displays a transparency showing sentence fragments taken from anonymous students' writing. Students collaborate with the teacher's support in applying the strategy they observed in order to identify and revise the sentence fragments.
- For cooperative practice, students work in pairs, students peer-edit their drafts, focusing on revising their sentence fragments. They investigate their writing in order to identify redundant patterns and categorize them as fragments, complete sentences, or clauses.
- Students continue to monitor and self-correct their writing when working independently.

Explicit Transactional Mediation of Spelling

Within the framework of explicit transactional mediation, teachers can shift from what Gentry and Gillet (1993) referred to as a simplistic approach to teaching spelling by memorization to a problem-solving approach that allows teaching spelling as the complex process it is.

The following five strategies framed by Sandra Wilde (1992) can be modeled and applied across the curriculum:

- Asking another person how to spell a word
- Using a placeholder so that the creative act of writing can continue knowing the word is not spelled correctly
- Using resources such as wall charts, dictionaries, texts, and electronic media
- Monitoring and revising spelling based on the consideration of several plausible options and the application of a growing knowledge of phonetic generalizations and word patterns
- Automatically spelling words that have been learned (pp. 99–118)

Because the emergence of spelling proficiency is a developmental process, the teacher's observation and assessment of student demonstrations form the basis for the explicit transactional mediation.

Weaver (1996) makes the following clarifying points about the teacher's role in the transactional model for learning the conventions of print. The teacher

- Serves as advocate rather than adversary, as editor rather than a critic thereby avoiding the error hunt.
- Promotes acquisition and use of grammatical constructions through reading and reading to students.
- Explains aspects of grammar, usage, and punctuation, minimizes grammatical terminology, maximizes examples, and avoids memorization.
- Emphasizes the production of effective sentences rather than analysis.
- Teaches not only "correct" punctuation but teaches effective punctuation based on examination of published texts.
- Leads discussions and investigating questions of usage instead of doing usage exercises. (pp. 26, 84)

A Thought

Each time you are in possession of your students' writing and you find yourself reaching for a correcting pen, red or otherwise, it helps to have a note within view. Nothing too big, just a small piece of paper with a brief message, "It's the writer, not the writing!" I find that works for me and helps to keep my students in the driver's seat where they are in position to guide their own writing.

8

LOOKING UNDER THE HOOD:
KEY PROBLEM-SOLVING BEHAVIORS

Over the years I often saw students who were studies in incongruity—eager to learn, engaged, inventive, and inquisitive yet struggling with the management and execution of their classroom assignments for which they generally received poor grades. Whether they were copying board work, doing two-place multiplication, looking back in their books to find the stages in the life of a spider, or writing a comparison of frogs and toads, the products of their efforts were often incomplete, inaccurate, or missing in action. Like Jekyll and Hyde, these students presented two faces. When they were initiating a response based in their own fund of information or their original thoughts, they were astute and insightful. It was when they were asked to process information presented to them that they floundered.

When I was introduced to Reuven Feuerstein's (1980) landmark book *Instrumental Enrichment: An Intervention Program for Cognitive Modifiability,* which charted the territory of deficient cognitive functions, I found the language I needed to process and understand what I was seeing in those students:

> All too often, a child's failure to perform a given operation, whether in the classroom or in a test situation, is attributed either to a lack of

knowledge of the principles involved in the operation or, even worse, to a low intelligence that precludes his understanding of the principles. What is overlooked is that the deficiency may reside not in the operational level or in the specific content of the child's thought processes but in the underlying functions upon which the successful performance of cognitive operations depends. For example, underlying the operation of classification are a number of functions such as systematic and precise data gathering, the ability to deal with two or more sources of information simultaneously, and the necessity to compare the objects or events to be classified. . . . Clearly, a failure to locate the source of a child's errors will seriously affect the efficacy of any corrective action on the part of teachers or psychologists. (p. 71)

Feuerstein assigned poor cognitive functioning to four categories:

- **Impairments in cognition at the *input phase*.** The student's perceptions of information are blurred and sweeping. His exploration of the material is unplanned, impulsive, and unsystematic.
- **Impairments in cognition at the *elaborational phase*.** The data available to the student are used inefficiently. He is unable to select relevant versus irrelevant cues in defining a problem.
- **Impairments in cognition at the *output phase*.** The student cannot adequately communicate the outcomes of his efforts. He provides trial-and-error or egocentric responses that lack precision and accuracy.
- **Affective-motivational factors.** The student's negative attitudes impair cognitive processes.

The hallmark of Feuerstein's work with cognitively impaired students was the demonstration that these behaviors are modifiable with carefully articulated mediation.

The early writings of Costa and Lowery (1989) on intelligent behaviors, now termed habits of mind (Costa & Kallick, 2000, 2008, 2009), helped me to visualize how I could mediate the behaviors that underlie the cognitive impairments Feuerstein articulated. I knew that many students in the general population had these same difficulties to a lesser degree. I realized that the following behaviors are an integral part of each level of information processing:

- Thoroughness, accuracy, and impulsivity control
- Flexibility
- Persistence

Thoroughness, Accuracy, and Impulse Control: Strategy Anatomy

What do we observe when students do not have internal strategies for executing tasks with thoroughness and accuracy? Feuerstein characterizes the behavior we observe as blurred and sweeping perception. Specifically, the students' responses to their reading and their search for answers produce few details. They lack clarity as to what they are looking for and where to find it.

Impulsiveness, usually a key factor here, is characterized by unplanned and unsystematic exploratory behavior. When presented with many cues, the student's scanning is disorganized, and she is unable to select specific attributes relevant to a solution. When asked, she has a poor definition of the problem and lacks clear goal orientation. When an answer is produced, it is based on one piece of information because she has stopped exploring prematurely. There is no awareness of the need for additional data. The impulsive student takes an accidental approach to completing tasks and makes arbitrary selections. This behavior impacts a student's ability to follow directions because by responding to the first piece of information and not waiting for all the available data, the student cannot integrate all the necessary data needed for the task.

How can we mediate the lack of thoroughness, accuracy, and impulse control? Which task would be a good vehicle for analysis of those behaviors? Which skills would be suitable for explicit instruction? We have any number of options. Whether fixing a broken toy, washing your hands before eating, hitting a ball with a bat, conducting a science experiment, practicing a piece of music on an instrument, reporting an accident, or researching a topic, thoroughness, accuracy, and impulse control are critical to the outcome. The steps we take to avoid error are fundamentally the same.

Select a task you would have to be thoughtful about in order to avoid making a mistake. When you are finished listing the steps you took to be thorough and accurate while doing that task, you could compare your list with the one below. I selected a ubiquitous study skill to analyze—locating an answer to a question. (See Chapter 10, Social Studies Workshop, for the model lesson.)

• Clarify objective by underlining key question words and paraphrasing the task.
  • Decide on an appropriate pace to work at.
  • Plan.
  • Refocus on the objective.
  • Be systematic—don't jump around.
  • Verify—reread and double check.
  • Don't skip anything that is relevant to the task.
  • Verify.

During practice activities, students reinforce the use of these strategies. They learn to put space and time between the input and output phase of responding to a task. Feedback from teacher and peers during mediation helps impulsive students build awareness of productive practices and replace ineffectual habitual behaviors. Because the transactional mediation model repeatedly places the learner in interactive settings, students develop verbal skills that are critical to understanding, processing, and elaborating information. As Feuerstein (1980) explains, verbal abstractions such as terms for commonality or difference, relational terms, and labeling generalizations are critical for turning operations into a more universal key in solving similar problems.

Demonstrations of the Need for Mediation

In assessing students' needs for mediation in this area of cognitive functioning, we want to make the distinction between casual and occasional omissions in students' reading and writing responses and pervasive patterns such as these:

• Approaches reading in an episodic way (each object or event is experienced in isolation), not considering available information in order to make connections with prior knowledge and anticipate the content of the text

- Does not raise questions, make inferences, or engage in fix-up strategies when reading; shows little or no awareness of perplexities in the text or discrepancies between the reader's knowledge and the text
- Does not try to actively generate information by organizing, summarizing, or comparing events in order to place them in a larger, more meaningful context
- Does not gather and use information from more than one source when answering questions; limits attention to simple identification and does not engage in relational thinking such as inferring, comparing, summarizing, and synthesizing
- Has difficulty understanding and implementing classifying strategies that improve the focus, organization, and elaboration of written ideas
- Cannot verbalize the reasons for his choice of words or sentences
- Does not use words that generalize and connect ideas
- Self-corrects errors in spelling, grammar, punctuation, and capitalization when prompted to do so
- Completes assignments quickly regardless of their complexity or difficulty

Activities for Assessing Thoroughness, Accuracy, and Impulsive Behavior
- Reading response journals
- Written responses to reading
- Narrative and expository writing
- Letter writing
- Literature circles
- Guided reading activities
- Mathematical problem solving
- Homework assignment
- Following directions

Flexibility and Persistence

WD-40, the petroleum based lubricant and protectant created for the space program, was invented by John S. Barry in 1953. The *WD* stands for "water displacement." It took 40 attempts to work out the winning formula. The product was first used to protect the outer skin of the Atlas missile from rust and corrosion.

Since then it has found its way into as many as 80 percent of American homes and has at least 2,000 uses. Clearly the invention of WD-40 is a story of thoroughness and accuracy, but it is also a story of persistence and flexibility.

If John S. Barry were not striving for accuracy, no amount of persistence and flexibility would have helped him succeed. He needed to pay attention to the details of his chemical formulations. He had to keep careful records of how the combinations of chemicals were interacting; he had to make generalizations, draw conclusions, and plan further action based on these observations. If he could not be flexible and think of another adjustment or another possibility once he failed to get the desired result, all his accurate calculations would not have mattered. All his accurate and flexible behavior would not have been significant if he was not persistent and he had given up on trial 3 or trial 15 or trial 39.

Strategy Anatomy for Flexibility

It is not as if the students who appear at our sides seeking help with the frequency and insistence of trains arriving in Grand Central Station do not know how to be flexible when faced with a problem. If a cookie were out of reach in the kitchen, chances are they would think of something to do besides standing on their toes. Motivation cannot be discounted as a factor in initiating flexible behaviors. However, mediation that teaches students a repertoire of flexible behaviors and the awareness that not knowing how to solve a problem is where the work starts, not stops, can change every aspect of their performance in and out of school.

What do you do when you are flexible? What strategies do you engage in when you try to figure out the familiar phrase represented by the following Wacky Wordy?

- Verbalize what you observed.
- Change terms; use synonyms (circles, 0's, round shapes, zeros).
- Reverse direction—work backward (First try: over, above, on top. Then try: under below, beneath).
- Review what you have done.
- Eliminate what has not worked.

- Shift attention to a different part of the problem.
- Simplify (instead of "six *i*'s," just "*i*'s").
- Other strategies not used here are to extremize, categorize, and analogize.

Explicit transactional mediation of behavior lacking in flexibility enables teachers to address the many obstacles that interfere with this disposition of learning and problem solving. Students who have difficulty considering information from two or more sources are not able to consider alternative points of view. Working alongside teacher and peers, they see that behavior modeled and hear the strategy verbalized.

Because flexibility is valued by teacher and peers, students who are not able to accept that their answer is not the only answer or the correct answer, have many opportunities to observe that changing one's mind or one's course of action in the face of new data is considered intelligent behavior. Such behavior would ultimately lead to translating the Wacky Wordy above to "circles under the eyes."

Demonstrations of the Need for Mediation

The following behaviors are characteristic of students who do not have strategies of problem solving with flexibility:

- Does not attempt to word solve in more than one way
- Gives up trying to resolve difficulty understanding words or sentences
- Does not adjust thinking after reading new information that challenges the accuracy of their original response
- Resists or refuses to revise writing
- Does not compromise in order to resolve conflicts
- Can only state one way to solve a problem

Activities for Assessment of Flexibility

- Responses to literature
- Oral reading
- Group discussions
- Cooperative activities
- Problem solving across the curriculum
- Responding to feedback in writers' workshop

Strategy Anatomy for Persistence

Persistence without flexibility has a figurative equivalent: it is also known as banging your head against the wall. So when we teach for persistence we would be doing a disservice to our students if we do not give them the tools for adjusting and changing their approach to the problem. Persistence, therefore, is not a matter of repeating a behavior over and over and hoping one of these times soon what we are doing is bound to work. It requires strategizing, analyzing, and developing a system or a new structure for attacking the problem. The work that persistence requires is energized by accruing additional knowledge while in the process of trying to succeed.

When analyzing persistent behavior really give yourself a challenge. Those interconnected metal puzzle pieces gave me a lot of insight into persistence. Notice the difference between doing a task you expect to be able to master as opposed to one that seems out of reach.

What is the work of persistence?

- Distinguish exactly what is not working.
- Think about other options that are available to you.
- Prioritize those options. Start with the one that addresses the problem most directly.
- Decide if there is an adjustment that could be made within the strategy that did not work.
- Eliminate the strategies that have not worked.
- Think outside the box. Use models, examples, and resources that would shed light on the problem.
- Approach the problem by simplifying the data.
- Substitute challenging words and concepts with the familiar—analogizing the problem.
- Draw, diagram, note, list, or map the information you are working with.

Demonstrations of Persistent Behavior

- Staying with a problem before asking for assistance
- Expressing pride in finding solutions and clearing up confusion
- Continuing to use word-solving behaviors during oral reading even though the teacher is available for support

- Writing revisions that reflect repeated efforts to find the "right" words
- Being energized by problem-solving tasks instead of feeling frustrated and resentful
- Verbalizing the strategies that can be used when stuck
- Seeing the value and necessity of working on solving authentic problems and seeking answers for an extended period of time

Activities for Assessing Persistence

- Oral reading
- Extended written responses to reading
- Scientific experimentation to resolve inquiries
- Challenging mathematics problems
- Writing conferences to improve focus, organization, language, and clarity

A Final Word About Key Problem-Solving Behaviors

Wouldn't it be sufficient to teach reading and writing strategies that require accuracy, flexibility, and persistence? By showing the many ways to unlock a word or a word's meaning, aren't we demonstrating flexible behavior? By demonstrating how to proofread or check a math computation, aren't we modeling standards of thoroughness and accuracy? When we guide students through a complicated, problem-ridden project, aren't we teaching persistence?

These are fitting questions for our last section on key cognitive behaviors because they return us to the issue at the core of bringing about improvement and change: explicit mediation. Our efforts and our aspirations for our students require that we nudge our way into that space between the learner and the learning. That is where we can label, define, demonstrate, connect the new with what is known, provide opportunities for students to select strategies and apply them to diverse problem-solving situations. It is through our explicit coaching, teaching, and support that we build a value system around knowing what to do when you don't know.

9

SETTING THE STAGE

Setting the Stage for Parents

Just when I was ready to take the plunge and bring my new mediation strategies to my students, I detected a faint voice coming through my planning mind. I paid attention and realized I was hearing Arthur Costa's voice. He was telling a group of teachers and administrators, at a summer conference I attended, the importance of bringing parents along when making a paradigm shift and initiating change in the classroom. If you don't, he admonished, our well-conceived, heartfelt initiative could be doomed for failure.

I realized that parents would need to be aware of our dual agenda, so I communicate the following key points to them early in the school year during school visits and through online communication:

1. Our ultimate goal is to empower children by teaching them to be self-guided, confident learners.

2. Your child will be learning the strategies that highly effective and proficient readers, writers, and problem solvers use, as well as the content of the curriculum.

3. The investment we make in teaching strategies will support and improve your child's performance on assessments.

4. You will need to learn the language of your child's work, such as *metacognition, think-aloud, mapping, monitoring, rubric,* and the names of the key strategies.

5. I invite you to partner with me in giving your child positive feedback and reinforcement for using the strategies I am teaching in the classroom.

6. To support your children's efforts, you may need to learn some new behaviors of your own, such as allowing wait time for decoding and problem solving, prompting your child to think aloud, and using graphic representations such as semantic maps to clarify ideas and information.

7. I will need your ongoing feedback, perspective, and questions in order to evaluate your child's use of the strategies being taught. We need to work together to find the most comfortable and convenient ways to sustain communication.

Setting the Stage for Students

Those of us who came of age in classrooms that practiced teaching by transmission (which is most of us regardless of our age) need to make a conscious effort to view our students as original sources as opposed to empty vessels. Working in a constructivist paradigm, we need to set the stage for explicit strategy instruction by researching our students' attitudes and understanding. We have to ask the questions that will reveal our students' beliefs about intelligence, learning, and what it takes to get better at what you do. The following questions can be used to launch that dialogue:

- What do you think it means to be intelligent? Why?
- How do you think a person gets to be intelligent? Why?
- Do you think you are an intelligent person? Why?

To encourage students to reflect on these questions, ask them to journal or map their answers independently before responding aloud in a group discussion. You want to have an understanding of each student's schema around the concept of intelligence.

To lay the groundwork for our mission, it is important that students understand the following:

1. Cognitive psychologists can now see into our brains with magnetic imaging devices. The research these scientists have done has taught us a lot about what happens in the brain when we think. (Use the Internet to show MRI images.)

2. We now know that our brains change. The more we think, the better we become at thinking. (You can demonstrate this point by showing pictures of dendrite growth that results from learning and thinking; see Figure 9.1.)

3. Many researchers have proven that we can actually be taught to be more intelligent. We can learn what to do when we don't know.

Figure 9.1 | **Dendrite Growth**

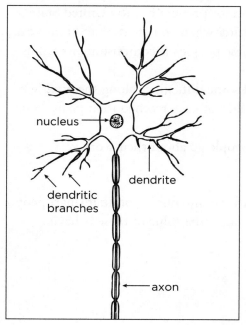
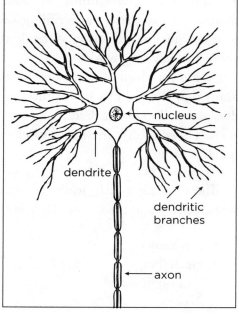

4. Researchers have learned which behaviors very successful people use when they read, write, and problem solve.

5. As a community of learners, we are going to learn and practice those important behaviors when we read, write, and solve problems. We can build a repertoire or tool box of strategies that enable us to behave intelligently and effectively.

I have limited our focus to four critical behaviors. Costa and Kallick give us an in-depth and comprehensive understanding of how to teach 16 important habits of mind in their books *Learning and Leading with Habits of Mind* (2008) and *Habits of Mind Across the Curriculum* (2009).

The following questions, which can be modified for age and interest levels, can be used to elicit just what habits of mind we want to have:

1. What qualities do you think Bill Gates, Tiger Woods, Barack Obama, William Shakespeare, J. K. Rowling, and Helen Keller share despite their very different fields of expertise? Why?

2. Do you think that developing new computer technology, becoming a champion athlete, winning the election for president of the United States, writing a masterpiece, or becoming a writer when you are deaf and blind can be done quickly and easily? What do these people's accomplishments tell us about the way they work?

3. Do you think they may have had some difficulties along the way? We know they did not give up, or they would not have reached their goals. What does that tell us about them?

4. Do you think these exceptional people go about their work very quickly? Why?

These questions help students discard the misconception that smart people work quickly and finish fast. They illuminate the value of these behaviors:

• Persistence
• Flexibility
• Thoroughness
• Accuracy

I like to make a list of the behaviors my class is focusing on and keep it prominently displayed. I want my students to understand the relevance these behaviors have to their own lives. To make that connection, I want them to ponder and discuss questions such as these:

1. Would you go to a doctor who is not persistent to treat you for an illness? Why?

2. Would you want a pilot who is not accurate to fly the plane you take to Florida? Why?

3. Would you want a carpenter who is not thorough to build your house? Why?

I emphasize that as a community of learners we are going to be focusing on both the subjects we study and the habits of mind that grow intelligence.

Setting the Stage for Teachers

I have come to regard the explicit teaching of a key strategy as my "Moses moment." I gather my students unto me. I want to captivate my audience with all the drama and wisdom I can summon so that when they disperse they leave with new understanding, clarity of purpose, and the intention to go forth and apply what they have learned.

Melodrama aside, the lesson I am presenting is nothing less than a key strategy—a set of behaviors that are essential for proficiency in reading, writing, or thinking. It deserves nothing less than my careful preparation and my students' rapt attention. We have to thank Lucy Calkins for the wisdom of demonstrating a specific behavior as though in a pregame huddle. Gathering my students around me, whether on a carpet or in a meeting area in the classroom, is a commanding way to signal that something special is about to take place. As we have pointed out, cognitive psychologists tell us that if you want your students to attend, it is helpful to create a strong contrast from what you were just doing.

Asking students to leave their seats and come together in close proximity, literally and symbolically, transforms students into a community within the community of the classroom. When we are in a community, we must enter a contract for the good of the group that articulates expectations and defines consequences. For example, transitioning from desk to gathering place must be done quickly and purposefully. Only materials I have asked for should be brought to the meeting. The classroom code of consequences for interfering with others' ability to concentrate applies to the workshop, too.

I am "on stage," so I use my voice for dramatic effect. My tone and intonation can pull my students in and convey my enthusiasm for what is about to take place. I try to craft my words for economy and purpose. My posture, leaning into my students and maintaining eye contact, eliminates the need to tell them how important my message is.

My lesson, the explicit teaching of a key strategy, is my show and tell. I engage my students by asking questions initially, but the teaching mode is modeling. As such, I am not delivering a lecture, nor am I inviting recitation or regurgitation. I am not coaching or coaxing. I am showing what I do and thinking aloud.

Subsequent to the explicit lesson, when I model problem solving, I want to reveal my own road blocks and mishaps rather than the "perfect reasoning" of the expert. I want my students to see me in the act of not knowing, and then I want them to see what I do when I don't know. When I hear my students echoing those behaviors while metacogitating and conferencing with fellow students, I know they have begun to internalize the models I have presented.

A BIRD'S-EYE VIEW

10

This chapter provides a snapshot of the explicit teaching we have been describing when it is embedded in the larger context of a day in the life of a classroom. This perspective will allow us to see how the teaching of a cognitive behavior can be integrated with lessons across the curriculum and how the commitment to self-guided learning can be maintained regardless of the content. As you will see, the workshop (as informed by Fountas & Pinnell, 2001) is the hub from which the amalgamation of activities and lessons presented in this chapter emanate. It is, in a sense, the natural habitat for mediation that is transactional, dynamic, and differentiated.

The Reading Workshop

Explicit Strategy Instruction

The reading workshop is underway in Ann Daley's 4th grade classroom. This morning Ann is launching the study of an important reading strategy. The entries in the students' reading response journals and the observations she has made during literature discussions demonstrate that many of her students have difficulty remembering what they read. They need to reread in order to respond to the text, and their recall is sketchy and incohesive. The absence of indented paragraphs in the students' writing confirms her supposition that many of them have not developed an awareness of the organization of text. Several strategies can address her students' poor recall, such as visualizing, questioning, and predicting. However, Ann has decided to begin mediation by teaching her students to summarize or chunk information while they are reading. Organizing ideas is central to understanding and remembering. She decides to make this core strategy the focus for the explicit strategy lesson of her next reading workshop. Her lesson is based on the analysis she did of the steps we take when we organize text.

When everyone is gathered, Ann begins by telling her class that sometimes when she is reading, she gets to the bottom of the page and realizes she doesn't really remember what she read. Ann asks the students if that ever happens to them, and there is a silent chorus of nods. She adds that this is particularly true when she is reading something she isn't really that interested in. This last statement generates enthusiastic agreement and knowing smiles. She tells her students she is going to show them one way she helps herself understand and remember what she reads.

Ann explains that understanding and remembering is always easier when we put things together and organize them in some way. She reaches into a plastic bin beside her chair and takes out a box of assorted blocks, which she dumps out on the table in front of her. She asks the students if they would be able to describe what is in the pile. "Can you tell how many colors there are? Is it clear if there are more red ones or green ones? How many blocks are there all together?" She asks them what they would do to make the pile clear and easy to understand. Ann tells the students, all of whom have already raised their hands, eager to reply, to turn to a neighbor and share their answers with each other.

After the class has shared their ideas and agreed that they would organize the blocks, Ann invites her students to put their hypothesis to the test. Students take turns separating and organizing the blocks by their shared characteristics. Ann smiles to herself over the wonder of kids in the video age clamoring to get their hands on a few blocks.

When the matched blocks are arrayed in columns, Ann emphasizes the difference organization makes by asking some questions that require gathering information and making comparisons the students could not have made when the blocks were in one big pile. She relates these observations to other places in and out of their homes where objects are organized, such as rooms, drawers, libraries, and supermarkets. She would extend the experiences with manipulative materials if the students' ages or cognitive ability warranted it.

Ann then tells her students that we can also group or chunk information in the text we are reading to help us understand and remember. She instructs her class to watch and listen as she "chunks" the familiar story of Goldilocks and the Three Bears. She tells them that because they know the story, she is going to tell it very quickly, and when she is finished, she will ask them to tell her what they observed.

Ann picks up a marker and places a stack of 6″ × 8″ index cards in front of her. Speaking quickly, Ann tells the story; however, when the tale transitions from one scene to the next, she stops and exclaims, "Wait a minute. That sounds like a new episode is starting. It's a new scene. It's different from what was happening before. Let me stop there and think about what I found out." She reviews the details and asks, "What are all those details talking about?" Ann thinks aloud as she makes the connection. Then she writes a summarizing sentence on an index card, such as "Goldilocks goes into the bears' house and helps herself to the porridge."

When Ann has finished modeling the "chunking" of the story and has placed the index cards on display, she asks the students to retell what they observed. She records the strategy on chart paper. Then she asks her students to think, pair, and share the answers to these questions: What are we doing? Why are we doing it? While the students are responding, she circulates and listens for their ability to articulate what they are learning and makes notes regarding which students need more time, coaching, and practice to process the concept of chunking.

Following the group share, Ann prepares her students for the transition into two groups—one will receive guided practice in summarizing text and the other high-ability group will resume work in their literature response circles.

Guided Practice

Ann's teaching is grounded in her commitment to enable her students to be self-guided learners. The structure of her program, the nature of her interactions with her students, and her responses to their challenges are always geared to build their awareness of the behaviors they need to succeed and to release control of those behaviors to her students.

The guided reading portion of the reading workshop puts her students in the driver's seat as soon as they are aware of what they need to do and have an understanding of the processes needed to do it. Therefore, instead of preparing students for their reading by guiding their predictions, clarifying new vocabulary they will encounter, and anticipating the literary devices the author uses, Ann asks the students to apply the strategies she has modeled and select the behaviors that will serve their purposes before, during, and after reading. She provides support by coaching her students through the challenges that arise.

The students who have demonstrated a need to improve their recall remain in the gathering place with Ann. She tells them that they are going to work together to get practice in organizing or chunking a story. She has picked a piece of material that is well within their independent reading level. After briefly reviewing the strategy, the students in the group take turns reading aloud and stopping when they think a new episode or chunk has started. When there is a difference of opinion, Ann encourages a dialogue over the decision process, knowing that the separation of the episodes is not as important as the students' conscious attention to organizing information.

Before the students draw a picture representing the thrust of each episode along with a main-idea statement, Ann takes them through a rehearsal. She wants to mediate their processing of the text and encourage visualization. She asks, "What will be in your picture?" "Where will you place the characters?" She notes the students' ability to generalize ideas from the details. While her students are busy selecting markers and drawing, Ann checks in with each child by asking, "So could you teach me about what you are doing?"

When Ann and the students have finished collaborating on the chunking of the story, she has them reflect on the use of the strategy and ask any questions they may have. Ann tells her students they will have an opportunity to recall and discuss the story the next time they meet. At that time they will evaluate the use of the chunking strategy and she will give them feedback on the difference in their ability to remember what they read.

During the weeks to come, the guided reading blocks will move from teacher-directed activities to cooperative group activities and then independent work. Ann will model how to use the chunking strategy to demark episodes with highlighting tape, map a story, take notes, and summarize. She will ask the students to evaluate their recall and understanding and compare what they are doing now with what they used to do.

Literature Study

The literature study block of the reading workshop enables students to work in small groups and share their reactions to thought-provoking children's literature or informational text that will add dimension and perspective to their content-area investigations.

Ann is confident that she can balance the aesthetic enjoyment of reading good literature with instruction that builds expertise. She uses the extended text as a stage for the students to select and apply the strategies they have been learning. The global and interpretive questions she poses focus her class's attention on higher-level thinking, deep processing of information, and the search for meaning.

Ann joins the students who have been working in small collaborative circles on the books they have selected for literature study. After conferencing briefly with each group about their work and coaching students who ran into obstacles to their understanding, she gathers the small groups and poses the question, "What devices does the author use to hold your interest?"

She asks these more able students if they can apply the summarizing strategy to an analysis of their book's plot structure. They will need to identify the main episodes as they read and record them on 8″ × 10″ index cards. By attaching the sides of the cards with yarn, each group will construct a story line that reflects the rise and fall of tension in the plot. They will have to locate the literary devices the author uses to move the story along such as a disaster, surprise, suspense, uncertainty, fear, or tragedy. The groups can use their completed story lines for a book sharing with the whole class.

Language and Word Study

During the language–word study block, Ann extends her students' understanding of new vocabulary concepts taken from either the literature or expository material that they are reading. By framing these words in a semantic hierarchy map (see Figure 10.1), she constructs a definition of the word that includes its category, properties, and examples. The students work cooperatively to gather information from their reading to fill in the map.

Once the word being studied has been clarified, defined, and connected to the students' prior knowledge, Ann structures activities that require using the word with its proper connotation and in its proper context. Students place the word on the Word Study Wall so they can continue to make new connections and expand their schema around the word.

Figure 10.1 | **Semantic Word Map**

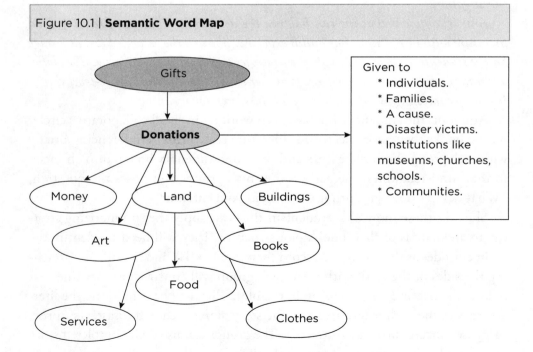

The Writing Workshop

Explicit Strategy Instruction

Ann launched her writing workshop at the beginning of the year wearing a construction hat and toting a tool box to dramatize the concept that writing is a building process. She asked the class to guess what tools would be inside a writer's tool box. For students who are not familiar with the writing process or writers' workshop, the scissors, tape, stapler, markers, glue, sticky notes, and highlighters that accompany the pencils, pens, and paper make the point that stories are constructed. Sometimes you decide you have to take something out, put something in, switch information around, or change what you have done. She wants her students to know the process takes time; books are not born fully formed.

Ann knows that the challenges her students have demonstrated around organizing narrative text will hamper their ability to understand and remember the more challenging expository material they read for content area studies and interfere with assembling research for their projects.

Because it is timely, Ann decides to devote her explicit instruction in the writing workshop to teaching her students strategies for organizing research material. She knows the strategies she teaches will be applied to the personal narratives her students are writing. She begins by sharing her plan with them and asking her class to discuss what strategies they think might be helpful in keeping the information they gather well organized and easy for their audience to understand.

Ann confirms that grouping or chunking information is a great idea. She asks her students to visualize cleaning up a very messy room, how they would take each item and add it to the place where the other similar items are kept. She says, "That's what we do when we gather research. Each piece of information has to be sorted and placed with other information that talks about the same thing." Since this is not a new concept, Ann does not introduce manipulative materials.

Ann tells her students she is going to model how she gathers information for her topic and how she organizes it before writing her report. She lets her class know that when she is finished, she is going to ask them to retell what she did.

Working on a white board, Ann writes her topic across the top and draws a large oval around it. She says, "I am going to make a map for myself before I write my report. My map will keep me from getting lost and disorganized. Everything I write below this big topic will belong to this topic or will be connected to it in some way. Just to remind myself of that connection, each time I add information I'll connect it to its topic with a connecting line." (See Figure 6.3 for a hierarchy map.)

Ann selects a reference that is appropriate for her topic and begins to read aloud and think aloud. She stops reading after a few sentences to reflect on what the information is talking about. Ann thinks aloud, "This information is relevant to my topic; it's talking about the weather conditions in the place I am researching. I'm going to connect a bubble to my topic labeled "weather." I'll list all the details for that subtopic below it." After Ann has gathered a good sample of information and modeled how she assigns the details she reads to a subtopic on her map, she stops and asks her students to retell what they observed so they can clarify and solidify the strategy she modeled.

Group practice in gathering and organizing information for writing will continue until Ann and her class decide that their research question has been answered. The students will continue to practice and apply the representational phase of organizing information (i.e., mapping) using their own topics and working first in cooperative groups and then independently. When the class has finished preparing their maps, Ann will model how to transform the map into a well developed research report starting with an introductory paragraph followed by well organized paragraphs consisting of topic sentences and supporting details. She has found that the use of a graphic organizer, as opposed to a Harvard outline, enables her elementary-level students to grasp and initiate the practice of organizing text.

Social Studies and Science Workshop

Ann uses a project-based approach for content-area learning. The hands-on, in-depth investigations of real-world topics engage her students' attention and effort. She knows from her experience with reading and writing workshops that when students are excited about what they are learning, they tend to dig more deeply, retain what they learn, make connections, and apply their learning to other problems.

Ann is circulating among the small cooperative learning groups that have been formed around a common interest. The projects have grown out of the central concept of interdependence. They have been seeking to understand how the health, safety, productivity, and education of people living far from them can affect their lives. The day Ann read Greg Mortenson's young reader edition of *Three Cups of Tea* to her class, the students decided they wanted to focus their projects on sending books to schools in places with high rates of illiteracy and poverty. A conversation ensued about the difference between making charitable donations and providing support that is empowering. The class decided that books support education and contribute to long-term improvement of living conditions for individuals, the community, and the world.

The students are at different stages of collecting and organizing the information they will need to send their donations to a school in a remote area. In conjunction with the class's focus on organizing information, Ann will stress the strategies that are needed for this complex project that will require researching; planning; communicating with businesses, nongovernmental organizations, community leaders, and schools; collecting; packaging; and shipping.

Test-Taking Seminar

Explicit Strategy Instruction

Ann includes test-taking strategies in the word study block of her reading and writing workshops. She wants her students to be aware that test taking requires a particular set of skills. Although the reading and writing experiences her students engage in prepare them for the tasks found on the state assessments and standardized tests, she knows that the format, test-taking conditions, and the language of test questions present challenges to her students that need to be addressed in order for them to achieve scores reflective of their competency. Ann teaches a test-taking strategy lesson as she does the other explicit strategy lessons.

The lesson begins with Ann telling her students they are going to learn a strategy for locating answers to questions on the reading assessments they will take in the spring. It is a strategy that will help them save time if they want to look back to verify or find an answer. This strategy will also require thorough and accurate behaviors.

Ann tells the class they could think of locating an answer in the way they would locate a treasure in a treasure hunt. She has asked a colleague to assist her by first hiding an object and then coming in to tell Ann and the class what she has hidden. Ann then tells the students to watch and listen as she models her strategy, reminding them she will ask them to retell what they observed.

Ann thinks aloud as she demonstrates her strategy for locating a hidden object she really wants to find. She models how she

1. Finds out what she will be looking for (*clarifies purpose*).
2. Thinks about where she could expect to find what she is looking for based on its use, size, thickness, and shape (*plans*).
3. Moves carefully, looks thoroughly, and does not jump around (*is systematic*).
4. Rereads the question (*refocuses*).
5. Searches persistently until there is no place left to look (*uses everything that is relevant to the task*).
6. Checks if the answer matches the question (*verifies*).

After reflecting on the strategy and listing the steps she took, Ann has her students practice the strategy they observed by dividing the class into small groups and staging a competitive treasure hunt. To qualify for a prize, the group has to plan their hunt strategy. If they conduct a random search, the group is disqualified.

In subsequent lessons, Ann applies the treasure hunt strategy to locating answers to test questions. She starts by reading aloud and chunking or summarizing the text. Then, she uses the organization of the material to decide where she will look for answers.

After the model lesson, students are asked to retell, reflect, and ask any questions they have about the strategy. Then Ann begins the process of providing scaffolded, transactional instruction in locating answers. While she uses the test practice booklets she is given, Ann embeds the practice and application of "test-taking" strategies in the classroom curriculum so that practicing the skills that are specific to test-taking does not replace meaningful reading and writing experiences.

Ann is confident that the richness of her language arts program, her attentiveness to her students' demonstrations of understanding, the student empowerment created by her gradual release of control, and the explicit transactional nature of the mediation provide ample preparation for the springtime assessments.

SUMMARIES OF MAJOR STUDIES ON EXPLICIT TRANSACTIONAL STRATEGIES INSTRUCTION

The five studies summarized here were chosen because they were conducted by eminent education researchers for the purpose of identifying and clarifying the teaching practices that lead to substantive achievement gains in reading and writing for a broad spectrum of students. Each of these important studies validates the efficacy of explicit and transactional cognitive strategy instruction.

National Institute of Child Health and Human Development. (2000). *Report of the National Reading Panel. Teaching children to read: An evidence-based assessment of the scientific research literature on reading and its implications for reading instruction.* Retrieved July 5, 2010, from http://www.nichd.nih.gov/publications/nrp/upload/smallbook_pdf.pdf

This report looks at the available research results on effective reading instruction in order to determine which practices for teaching phonemic awareness, vocabulary, and comprehension are ready for application in the classroom. The studies selected for review had to meet rigorous methodological research standards. The report's conclusions stem from the basic premise that "[r]eaders derive meaning from text when they engage in intentional, problem solving thinking processes" (p. 14). Some key points of the panel's report regarding comprehension include the following:

- The rationale for the explicit teaching of comprehension skills is that comprehension can be improved by teaching students to use specific cognitive strategies or to reason strategically when they encounter barriers to understanding what they are reading.
- Explicit or formal instruction in the application of comprehension strategies has been shown to be highly effective in enhancing understanding.
- The types of instruction that appear to have a solid scientific basis for improving comprehension in nonimpaired readers are comprehension monitoring, cooperative learning, graphic and semantic organizers, question answering and question generation, story structure, and summarization.
- When used in combination, these techniques can improve results in standardized comprehension tests.
- Transactional strategy instruction requires the teacher's ability to explain mental and cognitive processes explicitly and facilitate discussions of the processes involved in comprehension.
- When transactional strategy instruction has been successful, it has always been long-term, occurring over a semester or school year at minimum with consistent and striking benefits.

Hattie, J. (2009). *Visible learning: A synthesis of over 800 meta-analyses relating to achievement.* New York: Routledge.

Visible learning refers to learning variables that are supported by observable data. Using a synthesis of research studies judged to be well designed by research reviewers, Hattie averaged the effect sizes (ESs) for teaching and learning variables to arrive at the best guesses we have about what approaches have the greatest effect on student achievement. An ES of 0.4 is above average for educational research. An ES of 0.5 is equivalent to a one-grade leap. An ES of

1.0 is equivalent to a two-grade leap. Of all the variables measured, the following results were reported as "exciting":

Influence	Effect Size
Feedback	0.72
Teaching self-verbalization	0.67
Metacognition strategies	0.67
Teaching problem solving	0.61
Direct instruction	0.59

Direct instruction in this context refers to active learning in class, in which students' work is marked in class and they may do corrected work. There are reviews after 1 hour, 5 hours, and 20 hours.

Hattie states that self-regulation, the heart of visible learning and visible teaching, requires highly structured or direct teaching.

Pressley, M. (2001, September). *Comprehension instruction: What makes sense now, what might make sense soon. Reading Online, 5(2).* Retrieved April 25, 2010, from http://www.readingonline.org/articles/handbook/pressley/index.html

This article is part of a series drawn from work in the *Handbook of Reading Research: Volume III* (Kamil, Mosenthal, Pearson, & Barr, 2000). In this article, which is a follow-up to the chapter he wrote for the *Handbook,* Pressley discusses well-validated teaching practices and notes the concurrence of his conclusions with those of the National Reading Panel (National Institute of Child Health and Human Development, 2000). After articulating the research that supports transactional strategies instruction, he concludes

> The case is very strong that teaching elementary, middle school, and high school students to use a repertoire of comprehension strategies increases their comprehension of text. Teachers should model and explain comprehension strategies, have their students practice using such strategies

with teacher support, and let students know they are expected to continue using the strategies when reading on their own. Such teaching should occur across every school day, for as long as required to get all readers using the strategies independently—which means including it in reading instruction for years. (p. 5)

Pressley, M., & Harris, K. (2006). Cognitive strategies instruction: From basic research to classroom instruction. In P. A. Alexander & P. H. Winne (Eds.), *Handbook of educational psychology* (2nd ed., Chap. 12). New York: Routledge Taylor & Francis.

This comprehensive review of the literature on reading and writing instruction that has been demonstrated to improve achievement in a variety of student populations is a must for teachers and teacher educators. It showcases the striking results obtained from cognitive strategy instruction and Self-Regulated Strategies Development (SRSD).

The authors report that there are several very good evaluations of transactional strategies instruction (TSI). Brown, Pressley, Van Meter, and Schuder (1996) studied two 2nd grade student groups over the course of a school year. One received TSI and the other experienced conventional reading instruction.

Although at the beginning of the school year the two groups did not differ on any measures of reading achievement, by the end of the school year, the group that was taught comprehension strategies using the transactional approach outperformed control participants on a wide variety of quantitative and qualitative measures, including standardized test performance. The effects of a year of comprehension strategies instruction were consistent with the results reported by Anderson and others (Anderson, 1992; Brown et al., 1996; Duffy et al., 1987).

Pressley and Harris cite Wong and colleagues (1997, 2003) for their research on writing strategies with learning impaired secondary students. This work considered several critical principles in designing strategies instruction, including the affective needs of the students, and found an increase in the quality and quantity of students' writing. Wong and colleagues also noted that LD students needed more instruction and opportunities to write compared with their normally achieving peers.

Rosenshine, B. (1997, March 24–28). *The case for explicit, teacher-led, cognitive strategy instruction.* Paper presented at the annual meeting of the American Educational Research Association, Chicago. Retrieved March 9, 2009, from http://epaa.asu.edu/barak/barak1.html

Rosenshine makes the following summative points:

• We have 20 years of highly successful research on the development and teaching of cognitive strategies.

• For all expository reading, a study skill strategy that focuses on organizing and processing the material should be taught.

• The evidence to date has shown that students of all abilities, even high-achieving students, have benefited from being taught these cognitive strategies.

• The evidence does not support teaching the strategy only as the need arises, or only when the "teachable moment" arises, or using an on-the-spot instructional approach.

• As an example, the evidence from the reciprocal teaching studies shows that the format that began with teacher-led instruction in cognitive strategies yielded larger effect sizes than the format where the cognitive strategies were taught in the context of practice.

• The cognitive strategy research is very clear in support of explicit, teacher-led instruction in cognitive strategies.

Annotated Reference List

Other references on explicit transactional instruction worth noting.

Brown, R. (2008). The road not yet taken: A transactional strategies approach to comprehension instruction. *Reading Teacher, 61*(7), 538–547.

This article provides a detailed description of TSI, reports research on the difference between the instruction provided by TSI and non-TSI teaching, and explains how TSI can be integrated with current curriculum.

College of William & Mary, Department of Education. (2002). Explicit instruction for implicit meaning: Strategies for teaching inferential reading comprehension. *Considerations: Inferential Comprehension.* Retrieved July 5, 2009, from http://www.yellow documents.com/1316515-explicit-instruction-for-implicit. Available by order from http://education.wm.edu/centers/ttac/forms/considerations-packets-form.php.

This packet provides useful information about teaching inferential thinking using explicit instruction methods that are research based. Researchers found that students with high-incidence disabilities can learn to mediate their comprehension through intensive, systematic, and explicit strategy instruction.

Dulin, S. R. (n.d.). *From pits to passion: Does implementing transactional strategies instruction improve reading comprehension and enable a reader to move from an acclimated reader to a proficient reader?* Retrieved June 18, 2009, from http://www.bridgew.edu/Library/CAGS_Projects/Sdulin/litresearch.htm (Bridgewater University, Literacy Research)

This study contains a thorough review of transactional strategies instruction research and an extensive list that pertains to different student populations, standardized test results, decoding, and comprehension.

Englert, C. S., Raphael, T. E., & Anderson, L. M. (1992, March). Socially mediated instruction: Improving students' knowledge and talk about writing. *The Elementary School Journal, 92*(4), 411–449.

In Englert's influential studies of elementary students with and without learning disabilities, students improved their knowledge of writing process and their writing abilities with cognitive strategies instruction. LD students performed similarly to their normally achieving peers on all five post-test variables. Metacognitive knowledge was positively related to measures of performance, for both writing and reading.

Graham, K. R., & Harris, S. (2003). Students with learning disabilities and the process of writing: A meta-analysis of SRSD studies. In L. H. Swanson, K. Harris, & S. Graham (Eds.), *Handbook of learning disabilities* (pp. 323–344). New York: Guilford.

These researchers provide a large body of work with respect to all critical aspects of writing instruction and SRSD specifically. They document the significant and meaningful improvements produced by SRSD for normally achieving students as well as for students with learning disabilities.

Hilden, K. R., & Pressley, M. (2007). Self-regulation through transactional strategies. *Reading and Writing Quarterly, 23,* 51–75.

This informative study documented five 5th grade teachers in a yearlong professional development program. The study reported obstacles teachers faced and observed student growth in reading comprehension behaviors and self-regulation.

Housand, A., & Reis, S. M. (2008, Fall). Self-regulated learning in reading: Gifted pedagogy and instructional settings. *Journal of Advanced Academics, 20*(1), 108–136. Retrieved April 25, 2010, from http://www.eric.ed.gov/PDFS/EJ835870.pdf

In this qualitative study of a schoolwide approach to teaching self-regulated reading behaviors to gifted students, researchers focused on teacher-student interactions to investigate the environmental conditions in high- and low-SRL classrooms. Research results bear out the correlation between self-regulation and higher achievement and suggest that self-regulated learning can be improved with instructional methods and environmental conditions. These researchers also cite studies that concluded specific strategy instruction, when combined with modeling SRL strategies, increased comprehension more than modeling explicit strategies alone.

Huitt, W. (2008). Direct instruction: A transactional model. *Educational Psychology Interactive* (Valdosta State University). Retrieved April 25, 2010, from http://www.edpsycinteractive.org/topics/instruct/instevnt.html

This article provides a chart reflecting the repeated transactions of teachers and students during a TSI lesson. Citing research which found that explicit instruction generally produces better scores on standardized tests of basic skills than other approaches, the author shows how using a transactional model puts the focus of instruction on teacher and student interaction which is correlated with increased student achievement.

B

RATIONALE AND RESEARCH FOR THE COMPONENTS OF THE EXPLICIT TRANSACTIONAL MEDIATION MODEL

Educators with a focus on neuroscience, cognitive science, and educational research such as Renate and Geoffrey Caine, Leslie Hart, Eric Jensen, Marilee Sprenger, and Pat Wolfe have led the way in showing us how to teach with the brain in mind. The stock and trade of a teacher's craft—building concepts, expanding procedural knowledge, teaching for understanding, and improving attention, retention, and information retrieval—have been influenced by their work. This appendix describes how their writings inform the mediation practices discussed in this book.

Tell students which strategy you are going to teach.

Paying attention is not easy to do consciously. Neuroimaging methods show an increase in the neural firing in the frontal lobes when someone is working hard to pay attention. One effective way to compel learners to pay attention, orient, engage, and maintain the appropriate neural networks is task prediction. Students are successful at explicit learning when they can identify the cognitive patterns and procedural sequences of the material being taught (Jensen, 2005).

Explain or show why the strategy is important and useful to students.

When students are able to envision how lessons will make for positive and successful learning experiences, the lessons take on an emotional relevance for them. The short path between the thalamus and the amygdale ensures that we react quickly to emotionally relevant information. The brain attends first to information that has a strong emotional content, and it remembers this information longer (Wolfe, 2001).

Learning is also influenced by the commitment of the learner. People have the power to generate commitment at any time. The way we think about a task greatly affects how we approach the task. A learner's belief that intense, extended effort will generally lead to success is more important than the individual's belief in his or her ability to do a task (Marzano, 2003).

Clarify central concepts and make connections to students' prior knowledge.

Pattern recognition, the matching of new input to stored information, is a critical aspect of determining whether content is meaningful to us (Anderson, 1995; Caine & Caine, 1991; Wolfe, 2001). Relevance is one of the easiest, most commonly made types of meaning, and it takes place at the cellular level. A neuron that already exists "connects" with a nearby neuron. When incoming information is relevant, it can activate entire neural fields. The more associations your brain creates, the more neural territories are involved and the more firmly the information is woven in neurologically (Jensen, 2005). All learning and especially long-term learning is fundamentally influenced by prior knowledge (Sprenger, 1999).

Use visual aids or manipulative materials to demonstrate the use of a strategy.

Concrete objects impact learning in the following ways:

• One key component in the process that filters incoming stimulus and determines if we attend to a particular stimulus is whether the incoming stimulus is different from what we are used to seeing—whether it is novel.

Neuronal activity increases when stimuli are in contrast to what we are used to seeing (Jensen, 2005; Wolfe, 2001).

• Manipulative materials and visual representations enable us to conceptualize new information and grasp relationships and connections (Hart, 1983).

• Concrete experiences engage more of the senses and use multiple pathways to store and recall information (Wolfe, 2001).

• We can only focus on building one neural pathway at a time. Other new learning contaminates the memory process. When we use content-neutral subject matter (e.g., blocks, clay, string), students do not need to process and clarify new semantic information. Instead, they can focus on the strategy being taught (Jensen, 2005).

Model the strategy.

Demonstrations provide a powerful incentive to students to emulate what they have observed. They help learners value what is being taught (Weaver, 1996). Demonstrations engage the visual modality of learning. "The eyes contain nearly 70 percent of the body's sensory receptors and send millions of signals every second along the optic nerves to the visual processing centers of the brain. It is not surprising that the visual components of memory are so robust" (Wolfe, 2001, p. 152).

Think aloud articulating the process.

Biemiller and Meichenbaum (1992) observed that spontaneous planning and monitoring statements are crucial indicators of the degree to which a child is functioning with expertise in a specific situation. When we model thinking aloud, we foster the behavior itself.

Ask students to retell the steps of the process they observed.

In order for long-term learning and understanding to take place, students must have time to organize, integrate, and store new information. The capacity for learning is limited by the processing time the brain requires. The brain has several systems and structures that function as "surge protectors" (Jenson, 2005).

Before we ask students to apply what they have learned to new material, retelling gives them the opportunity to engage in the first of several levels of information processing. By reviewing and creating a written record of the steps in the process being taught, students begin to solidify a new and unfamiliar strategy.

Ask students to think-pair-share and write answers to the questions (1) "What strategy are you learning?" and (2) "Why are you learning it?"

Either you can have learners' attention, or they can be making meaning, but both cannot happen at the same time. Synapses strengthen when students get time for neural connections to solidify without the need to respond to other competing stimuli. During that time, cellular resources can be preserved and focused on critical synaptic junctions. Wolfe (2001) explains:

> Procedural as well as declarative memory requires a process of consolidation, a gelling or setting time during which newly formed memories gradually become more stable. We know that memory is not formed at the moment information is acquired; memory is not a simple fixation process. Rather, it is dynamic, with unconscious processes that continue to strengthen and stabilize the connections over days, weeks, months, and years. (p.125)

Think-pair-share and journaling allows for personal processing time.

Students share their responses with the class and receive feedback from classmates and the teacher.

The upper, front middle of the brain, known as the anterior cingulate, is automatically activated when there is a discrepancy between what was expected and what actually happened. The brain is designed to operate on feedback, both internal and external. The whole brain is self-referencing. It decides what to do based on what has just been done. Feedback-driven learning makes more accurate and complex connections because the neural networks become more efficient when individuals learn by trial and error (Jensen, 2005).

Effective feedback (i.e., feedback that addresses the qualities of the work and the processes used to do the work) is one of the greatest intrinsic motivators. Peer feedback is more motivating and useful than teacher feedback in getting lasting results (Jensen, 1998).

Students practice the target strategy with peer and teacher support.

Support enables students to work in what Vygotsky (1986) calls the "zone of proximal development": to work at things that are just a little beyond what the learner could manage alone (Weaver, 1996).

Collaboration between and among teachers and students seems to be the best way to help most students become competent and independent learners (Weaver, 1996). Students learn that they can try new things without risking a negative response. A feeling of psychological safety is key to fostering new behaviors and higher-level thinking (Caine & Caine, 1991).

Students practice the strategy in a small group without teacher support.

The Stanford research on "complex instruction" demonstrates that learning increases when students are jointly engaged in problem solving. There is a positive and critical link between verbal interaction and learning. Groups can trigger multiple ways of interacting and allow students to view content from multiple perspectives. Group discussion is an effective way of processing experience because each student can reconstruct what he or she is learning (Caine & Caine, 1991). Organizing students in learning groups, whether they compete with each other or not, has a powerful effect on learning (Marzano, Pickering, & Pollock, 2001).

Students use the target strategy independently.

The opportunity to take charge of new learning while working independently in a personally meaningful way is essential to the growth and expansion of our students' competence. What we call "active processing" allows students to review how and what they learned so that they can consolidate and internalize information in a personally meaningful, conceptually coherent way (Caine & Caine, 1991; Rosenshine, 1997).

The students apply the strategy to a reading, writing, or problem-solving task first in a whole group, then working cooperatively, and then independently.

Researchers stress the importance of students being able to activate their memory of the teacher's comments at the right time and then interpret them—turn them into "mental acts"—in order to solve a problem. If students do not know when to apply principles, concepts, and strategies, their knowledge remains inert.

Numerous studies confirm that effective learning requires that learners actively use knowledge to read for meaning, write with purpose, and solve problems so that they learn to recognize the general conditions in which to apply strategies and concepts. Solitary practice provides no guarantee that students will learn how to orchestrate isolated skills to achieve broader goals (Marzano & Kendall, 2008).

Transfer learning to new contexts.

The teacher teaches for transfer by prompting students to
- Engage in the selection of task-appropriate strategies.
- Use the strategies in different contexts across the curriculum beginning in a whole-group setting with teacher support, then transferring the use of the strategies to different contexts while working with cooperative groups, and then working independently.

Most students do not transfer learning without direct instruction. The implicit assumption in educational practice has been that transfer takes care of itself. A great deal of knowledge students acquire is inert or passive. Students do not transfer the knowledge to problem-solving contexts where they have to think about new situations. "Rather than expecting students to achieve transfer spontaneously, one 'mediates' the needed processes of abstraction and connection making" (Perkins & Salomon, 1988, p. 28).

BIBLIOGRAPHY

Anderson, J. R. (1995). *Learning and memory: An integrated approach.* New York: Wiley.

Anderson, V. (1992). A teacher development project in transactional strategy instruction for teachers of severely reading-disabled adolescents. *Teaching and Teacher Education, 8,* 391–403.

Beck, I. L., & McKeown, M. (1991). Conditions of vocabulary acquisition. In R. Barr, M. L. Kamil, P. Mosenthal, and P. D. Pearson (Eds.), *Handbook of reading research* (Vol. II): 789–814. Mahwah, NJ: Lawrence Erlbaum.

Beyer, B. K. (1985). Practical strategies for direct instruction in thinking skills. In A. L. Costa (Ed.), *Developing minds: A resource book for teaching thinking.* Alexandria, VA: ASCD.

Beyer, B. K. (2001). What research says about teaching thinking skills. In A. L. Costa (Ed.), *Developing minds: A resource book for teaching thinking.* Alexandria, VA: ASCD.

Biemiller, A., & Meichenbaum, D. (1992, October). The nature and nurture of the self-directed learner. *Educational Leadership, 49*(2), 75–79.

Bloom, B., & Broder, L. (1950). *Problem solving processes of college students.* Chicago: University of Chicago Press.

Bloom, B. S. (1986, February). Automaticity: The hands and feet of genius. *Educational Leadership, 43*(5), 70–77.

Brown, H. D. (2007). *Teaching by principles: An interactive approach to language pedagogy.* Upper Saddle River, NJ: Pearson.

Brown, R. (2008). The road not yet taken: A transactional strategies approach to comprehension instruction. *Reading Teacher, 61*(7), 538–547.

Brown, R., Pressley, M., Van Meter, P., & Schuder, T. (1996). A quasi-experimental validation of transactional strategies instruction with low-achieving second grade readers. *Journal of Educational Psychology, 88,* 18–37.

Caine, R. N., & Caine, G. (1991). *Making connections: Teaching and the human brain.* Alexandria, VA: ASCD.

Calkins, L. M. (1983). *Lessons from a child: On the teaching and learning of writing.* Exeter, UK: Heinemann.

Calkins, L. M. (1986). *The art of teaching writing.* Portsmouth, NH: Heinemann.

Cleary, B. (1983). *Dear Mr. Henshaw.* New York: Morrow.

College of William & Mary, Department of Education. (2002). Explicit instruction for implicit meaning: Strategies for teaching inferential reading comprehension. *Considerations: Inferential comprehension.* Available: July 5, 2009, from http://education.wm.edu/centers/ttac/forms/considerations-packets-form.php.

Costa, A. (Ed.) (1985). *Developing Minds: A resource book for teaching thinking.* Alexandria: ASCD.

Costa, A., & Kallick, B. (2008). *Learning and leading with habits of mind.* Alexandria, VA: ASCD.

Costa, A., & Lowery, L. F. (1989). *Techniques for teaching thinking.* Pacific Grove, CA: Midwest Publications.

Costa, A. L. (1989). *Techniques for teaching thinking.* Pacific Grove, CA: Midwest.

Costa, A. L. (2001a). Mediating the metacognitive. In A. L. Costa (Ed.), *Developing minds: A resource book for teaching thinking.* Alexandria, VA: ASCD.

Costa, A. L. (2001b). Teaching behaviors that enable student thinking. In A. L. Costa (Ed.), *Developing minds: A resource book for teaching thinking.* Alexandria, VA: ASCD.

Costa, A. L., & Garmston, R. J. (2002). *Cognitive coaching: A foundation for renaissance schools.* Norwood, MA: Christopher-Gordon.

Costa, A. L., & Kallick, B. (Eds.). (2000). Using questions to challenge students' intellect. In *Activating and engaging habits of mind.* Alexandria, VA: ASCD.

Costa, A. L., & Kallick, B. (Eds.). (2009). *Habits of the mind across the curriculum: Practical and creative strategies for teachers.* Alexandria, VA: ASCD.

Duffy, G. G., Roehler, L. R., Sivan, E., Rackliffe, G., Book, C., Meloth, M., Vavrus, L. G., Wesselman, R., Putnam, J., & Bassiri, D. (1987). Effects of explaining the reasoning associated with using reading strategies. *Reading Research Quarterly, 22,* 347–368.

Dulin, S. R. (n.d.). *From pits to passion: Does implementing transactional strategies instruction improve reading comprehension and enable a reader to move from an acclimated reader to a proficient reader?* Retrieved June 18, 2009, from www.bridgew.edu/Library/CAGS_Projects/Sdulin/litresearch.htm (Bridgewater University, Literacy Research)

Durkin, D. (1978–79). What classroom observations reveal about reading instruction. *Reading Research Quarterly, 14*(4), 481–533.

Englert, C. S., Raphael, T. E., & Anderson, L. M. (1992, March). Socially mediated instruction: Improving students' knowledge and talk about writing. *The Elementary School Journal, 92*(4), 411–449.

Feuerstein, R. (1980). *Instrumental enrichment: An intervention program for cognitive modifiability.* Glenview, IL: Scott Foresman.

Flavell, J. H. (1977). *Cognitive development.* Englewood Cliffs, NJ: Prentice Hall.

Fountas, I. C., & Pinnell, G. S. (2001). *Guiding readers and writers grades 3–6.* Portsmouth, NH: Heinemann.

Gazzaniga, M. S., Ivry, R. B., & Mangun, G. R. (1998). *Cognitive neuroscience: The biology of the mind.* New York: Norton.

Gentry, J. R., & Gillet, J. W. (1993). *Teaching kids to spell.* Portsmouth, NH: Heinemann.

Gladwell, M. (2008). *Outliers.* New York: Little Brown.

Goodman, K. S., Shannon, P., Freeman, Y., & Murphy, S. (1988). *The report card on basal readers.* Katonah, NY: Richard C. Owen.

Graham, K. R., & Harris, S. (2003). Students with learning disabilities and the process of writing: A meta-analysis of SRSD studies. In L. H. Swanson, K. Harris, & S. Graham (Eds.), *Handbook of learning disabilities* (pp. 323–344). New York: Guilford.

Hart, L. A. (1983). *Human brain and human learning.* White Plains, NY: Longman.

Hattie, J. (2009). *Visible learning: A synthesis of over 800 meta-analyses relating to achievement.* New York: Routledge.

Hilden, K. R., & Pressley, M. (2007). Self-regulation through transactional strategies. *Reading and Writing Quarterly, 23,* 51–75.

Housand, A., & Reis, S. M. (2008, Fall). Self-regulated learning in reading: Gifted pedagogy and instructional settings. *Journal of Advanced Academics, 20*(1), 108–136. Retrieved April 25, 2010, from http://www.eric.ed.gov/PDFS/EJ835870.pdf

Huitt, W. (2008). Direct instruction: A transactional model. *Educational Psychology Interactive* (Valdosta State University). Retrieved April 25, 2010, from http://www.edpsycinteractive.org/topics/instruct/instevnt.html

Hyerle, D. (2009). *Visual tools for transforming information into knowledge.* Thousand Oaks, CA: Corwin Press.

Jensen, E. (1998). *Teaching with the brain in mind.* Alexandria, VA: ASCD.

Jensen, E. (2005). *Teaching with the brain in mind* (2nd ed.). Alexandria, VA: ASCD.

Johnson, D. D., & Pearson, D. P. (1978). *Teaching reading vocabulary.* New York: Holt, Rinehart and Winston.

Kamil, M. L., Mosenthal, P., Pearson, P. D., & Barr, R. (Eds.). (2000). *Handbook of reading research (Vol. III).* Mahwah, NJ: Lawrence Erlbaum.

Keene, E. O., & Zimmerman, S. (1997). *Mosaic of thought: Teaching comprehension in a reader's workshop.* Portsmouth, NH: Heinemann.

Lowery, L. F. (2001). The biological basis of thinking and learning. In A. L. Costa (Ed.), *Developing minds: A resource book for teaching thinking* (pp. 175–180). Alexandria, VA: ASCD.

Marzano, R. J. (2003). *What works in schools: Translating research into action.* Alexandria, VA: ASCD.

Marzano, R. J. (2007). *The art and science of teaching.* Alexandria, VA: ASCD.

Marzano, R. J., & Kendall, J. S. (2008). *Designing and assessing educational objectives: Applying the new taxonomy.* Thousand Oaks, CA: Corwin Press.

Marzano, R. J., Pickering, D. J., & Pollock, J. E. (2001). *Classroom instruction that works: Research-based strategies for increasing student achievement.* Alexandria, VA: ASCD.

Marzano, R. J., Presseisen, B. Z., Jones, B. F., Suhor, C., & Brandt, R. S. (1988). *Dimensions of thinking: A framework for curriculum and instruction.* Alexandria, VA: ASCD.

Mortenson, G. (2009). *Three cups of tea: One man's journey to change the world . . . one child at a time* (young readers ed.). New York: Puffin Books.

Nagy, W. E. (1988). *Teaching vocabulary to improve reading comprehension.* Newark, DE: International Reading Association.

National Institute of Child Health and Human Development. (2000). *Report of the National Reading Panel. Teaching children to read: an evidence-based assessment of the scientific research literature on reading and its implications for reading instruction.* Retrieved July 5, 2010, from http://www.nichd.nih.gov/publications/nrp/upload/smallbook_pdf.pdf

Palincsar, A. S., & Brown, A. L. (1984). Reciprocal teaching of comprehension-fostering and monitoring activities. *Cognition and Instruction, 1*(2), 117–175.

Palincsar, A. S., & Brown, A. L. (1989). Instruction for self-regulated reading. In L. B. Resnick & L. E. Klopfer (Eds.), *ASCD 1989 Yearbook: Toward the thinking curriculum: Current cognitive research* (pp. 19–39). Alexandria, VA: ASCD.

Paterson, K. (1978). *The great Gilly Hopkins.* New York: Crowell.

Pearson, P. D., & Duke, N. K. (2002). Comprehensive instruction in the primary grades. In C. Collins Block & M. Pressley (Eds.), *Comprehensive instruction: Research-based best practices.* New York: Guilford.

Pearson, P. D., & Gallagher, M. (1983). The instruction of reading comprehension. *Contemporary Educational Psychology, 8,* 317–344.

Perkins, D. N. (2001). Thinking for understanding. In A. L. Costa (Ed.), *Developing minds: A resource book for teaching thinking.* Alexandria, VA: ASCD.

Perkins, D. N., & Salomon, G. (1988, September). Teaching for transfer. *Educational Leadership, 46*(1), 22–32.

Piaget, J., & Duckworth, E. (1973, October). Piaget takes a teacher's look. *Learning,* 22–27.

Pressley, M. (2001, September). Comprehension instruction: What makes sense now, what might make sense soon. *Reading Online, 5*(2). Retrieved April 25, 2010, from http://www.readingonline.org/articles/handbook/pressley/index.html

Pressley, M., El-Dinary, P. B., Gaskins, I., Schuder, T., Bergman, J., Almasi, L., & Brown, R. (1992, May). Beyond direct explanation: Transactional instruction of reading comprehension strategies. *Elementary School Journal, 92*(5), 513–555.

Pressley, M., & Harris, K. (2006). Cognitive strategies instruction: From basic research to classroom instruction. In P. A. Alexander & P. H. Winne (Eds.), *Handbook of educational psychology* (2nd ed., Chap. 12). New York: Routledge Taylor & Francis.

Pressley, M., & Hilden, K. R. (2006). Cognitive strategies. In D. Kuhm & R. Siegler (Eds.), W. Danson & R. Lerner (Series Eds.), *Handbook of child psychology: Vol. 2. Cognitive perception, and language* (6th ed.). Hoboken, NJ: Wiley.

Pressley, M., Wood, E., Woloshyn, V. E., Martin, V., King, A., & Menke, D. (1992). Encouraging mindful use of prior knowledge: Attempting to construct explanatory answers facilitates learning, *Educational Psychologist*, 27(1), 91–109.

Robinson, M. (1980). *Housekeeping*. New York: Farrar, Straus and Giroux.

Rosenshine, B. (1979). Content, time, and direct instruction. In *Research on teaching: concepts, findings, and implications,* P. Peterson and H. Walberg (Eds.). Berkeley, CA: McCutchan.

Rosenshine, B. (1997, March 24–28). *The case for explicit, teacher-led, cognitive strategy instruction.* Paper presented at the annual meeting of the American Educational Research Association, Chicago. Retrieved March 9, 2009, from http://epaa.asu.edu/barak/barakl.html.

Routman, R. (1991). *Invitations: Changing as teachers and learners K–12.* Portsmouth, NH: Heinemann.

Routman, R. (1996). *Literacy at the crossroads: Crucial talk about reading, writing, and other teaching dilemmas.* Portsmouth, NH: Heinemann.

Serafini, F. (2004). *Lessons in comprehension: Explicit instruction in the reading workshop.* Portsmouth, NH: Heinemann.

Sprenger, M. (1999). *Learning & Memory: The brain in action.* Alexandria, VA: ASCD.

Squire, L. R., & Kandel, E. R. (2000). *Memory: From mind to molecules.* New York: Scientific American Library.

Stahl, S. A., & Fairbanks, M. M. (1986). The effects of vocabulary instruction: A model-based meta-analysis. *Review of Educational Research, 56*(1), 72–110.

Steig, W. (1982). *Doctor De Soto.* New York: Farrar, Straus and Giroux.

Sternberg, R. J. (1985). *Beyond IQ: A triarchic theory of human intelligence.* New York: Cambridge University Press.

Thaler, M. (1989). *The teacher from the black lagoon.* New York: Scholastic.

Vygotsky, L. S. (1986). *Thought and language* (A. Kozulin, Trans.). Cambridge, MA: Harvard University Press.

Weaver, C. (1996). *Teaching grammar in context.* Portsmouth, NH: Boynton/Cook.

Wilde, S. (1992). *You kan red this: Spelling and punctuation for whole language classrooms, K–6.* Portsmouth, NH: Heinemann.

Whimbey, A. (1984, September). The key to higher order thinking is precise processing. *Educational Leadership, 42*(1), 66–70.

Wolfe, P. (2001). *Brain matters: Translating research into classroom practice.* Alexandria, VA: ASCD.

Wolff, T. (1989). *This boy's life: A memoir.* New York: Grove.

Wong, B. Y. L. (1997). Research on genre-specific strategies for enhancing writing in adolescents with learning disabilities. *Learning Disabilities Quarterly, 20*(2), 140–159.

Wong, B. Y. L., Butler, D. L., Ficzere, S. A., & Kuperis, S. (1997). Teaching adolescents with learning disabilities and low achievers to plan, write, and revise compare-and-contrast essays. *Learning Disabilities Research and Practice, 12*(1), 2–15.

Wong, B. Y. L., Harris, K. R., Graham, S., & Butler, D. L. (2003). Cognitive strategies instruction research in learning disabilities. In H. L. Swanson, K. R. Harris, & S. Graham (Eds.) *Handbook on Learning Disabilities* (pp. 383–402). New York: Guildford.

INDEX

Note: An *f* following a page number indicates a figure.